MIND TEASERS

Philip J. Carter & Kenneth A. Russell

D1411668

MIND TEASERS

Philip J. Carter & Kenneth A. Russell

STERLING

New York / London
www.sterlingpublishing.com

STERLING and the distinctive Sterling logo are registered trademarks of
Sterling Publishing Co., Inc.

Library of Congress Cataloging-in-Publication Data Available

4   6   8   10   9   7   5   3

Published by Sterling Publishing Co., Inc.
387 Park Avenue South, New York, NY 10016

This book is comprised of material from the following titles:
Challenging IQ Tests © 1998 by Philip J. Carter & Kenneth A. Russell
The Little Giant® Encyclopedia of IQ Tests © 2000 by Philip J. Carter & Kenneth A. Russell

© 2007 by Sterling Publishing Co., Inc.

Distributed in Canada by Sterling Publishing
c/o Canadian Manda Group, 165 Dufferin Street
Toronto, Ontario, Canada M6K 3H6
Distributed in the United Kingdom by GMC Distribution Services
Castle Place, 166 High Street, Lewes, East Sussex, England BN7 1XU
Distributed in Australia by Capricorn Link (Australia) Pty. Ltd.
P.O. Box 704, Windsor, NSW 2756, Australia

Designed by StarGraphics Studio

Sterling ISBN 978-1-4027-4795-3

For information about custom editions, special sales, premium and
corporate purchases, please contact Sterling Special Sales
Department at 800-805-5489 or specialsales@sterlingpublishing.com.

Contents

Intelligence Testers

Test 1

Which word below
is an antonym of SIGNIFICANT?

SERIOUS, TRIVIAL, ABSURD, QUIET, or SIMPLE

Test 2

What number should logically
replace the question mark?

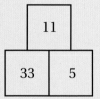 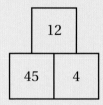 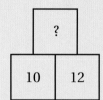

Test 3

ROTTEN LIAR is an anagram of what 10-letter word?

Test 4

Which is the odd one out?

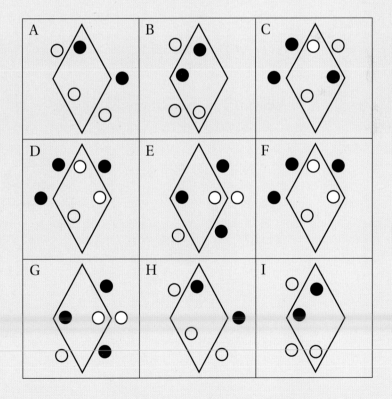

Test 5

At a recent small town election for mayor a
total of 963 votes were cast for the four candidates,
the winner exceeding his opponents
by 53, 79, and 105 votes, respectively.

How many votes were cast for each candidate?

300
247
221
195
963

Test 6

Pentag

What two nine-letter words can be formed
from the six three-letter bits below?

EVE, TAG, RED, PEN, RAM, LOP

Test 7

Change one letter in each word of
FIND ANY CANDY to make a well-known phrase.

Test 8

What two words that sound alike but are spelled differently mean AUDIBLY and PERMITTED?

Test 9

Fill in the blanks to make two words that are antonyms. The words spiral around the circle, one reading clockwise, the other reading counterclockwise.

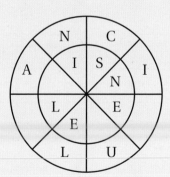

Test 10

LIBRA : SCALES ::

A. SAGITTARIUS : FISH
B. CANCER : TWINS
C. AQUARIUS : GOAT
D. CAPRICORN : BULL
E. ARIES : RAM

Test 11

What six-letter creature can be put in the boxes
to make three-letter words reading down?

N	A	E	W	F	O
E	T	R	A	E	W

Test 12

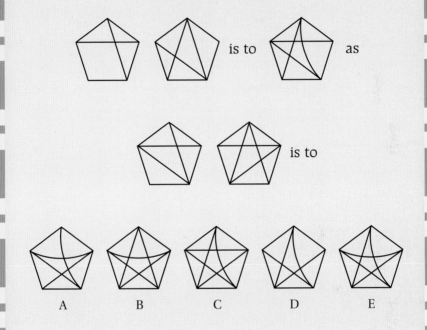

A   B   C   D   E

Test 13

Which two words below are closest in meaning?

GARGOYLE, WARLOCK, COCKATRICE,
HARRIDAN, BASILISK, SPRITE

Test 14

$6 + 7 \times 8 - 9 \times 2 = ?$

Test 15

Which of the following is not
an anagram of a type of building?

AIM DUST, RAY BIRL, AIM DRAG,
OIL PATHS, or VIOLA PIN

Test 16

What four-letter word can follow
the first word and precede the second
to make two new words or phrases?

SHOE, PIPE

Test 17

What shape is a CRINOID?

      A. CONE

      B. TULIP

      C. ARROW

      D. SHIELD

      E. LILY

Test 18

What number should logically replace the question mark?

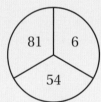 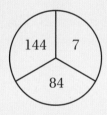 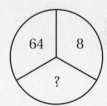

Test 19

Which two words below are opposite in meaning?

GRANDEE, DUKE, LESSEE,
SERVANT, LANDLORD, BUTLER

Test 20

Each line and symbol that appears in the
four outer circles above is transferred to
the center circle according to these rules:

If the line or symbol occurs in the outer circles
one time, it is transferred,
two times, it is possibly transferred,
three times, it is transferred, and
four times, it is not transferred.

Which of the circles below should appear
at the center of the diagram?

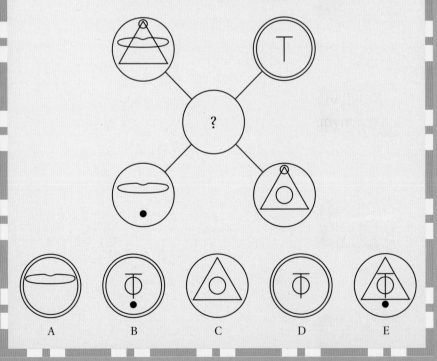

A   B   C   D   E

Test 21

Which number is the odd one out?

586414, 239761, 523377, 816184, 436564

Test 22

Combine two of the three-letter bits
below to make a small dog.
BEA, COL, RES, GLE, BOX, LIC

Test 23

Fill in the blanks to make two words that are
synonyms. The words spiral around the circle, one
reading clockwise, the other reading counterclockwise.

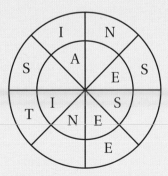

Test 24

SILLY TREES is an anagram
of what 10-letter word?

Test 25

What continues the above sequence?

A   B   C   D   E

Test 26

Which of the following is the missing segment?

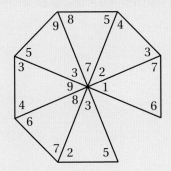

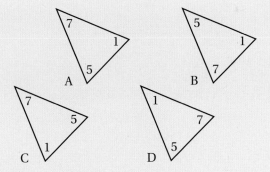

Test 27

$$76^2 - 75^2 = ?$$

Test 28

What two words that sound alike
but are spelled differently mean
MILITARY and ORGANIZE?

Test 29

What shape is FASTIGIATE?

A. TAPERING TO A POINT
B. OVAL
C. HEXAGONAL
D. BOTTLE
E. HOOK

Test 30

What continues the above sequence?

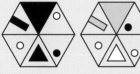

A   B   C   D   E

Test 31

What phrase is represented by the following?
Hint: Win some, lose some

FUNSTORE

Test 32

What number should logically replace the question mark?

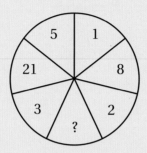

Test 33

Which is the odd one out?

OBOE, VIOLIN, TROMBONE, BASSOON, PICCOLO

Test 34

Which two words below are opposite in meaning?

SPLENETIC, FEVERISH, HAPPY,
MISGUIDED, DOMINEERING, POPULAR

Test 35

What nine-letter American city can be put in
the boxes to make three-letter words reading down?

H	S	G	H	T	Y	A	F	A
U	K	E	O	E	O	S	O	C

Test 36

CONVECTION : HEAT ::

A. MAGNIFICATION : SIGHT
B. ILLUMINATION : LIGHT
C. SPECTRUM : WAVELENGTH
D. VOLUME : SOUND
E. ANOSMIA : SMELL

Test 37

Which two words below are closest in meaning?

EGLANTINE, EGGLIKE, PATCHWORK,
BRIER, HEATH, CHANGELING

Test 38

What three-letter word can follow the first word and
precede the second to make two new words or phrases?

HOG, PIN

Test 39

586 : 46
374 : 25

Which numbers below have the same relationship
to one another as the numbers above?

A. 246 : 48
B. 319 : 13
C. 642 : 20
D. 913 : 28
E. 832 : 26

Test 40

Which circle should logically
replace the question mark?

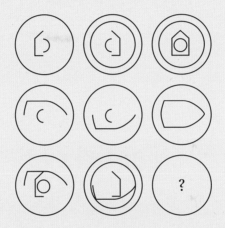

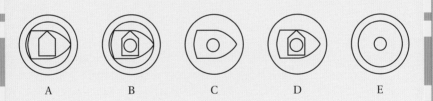

A   B   C   D   E

Test 41

What number should logically
replace the question mark?

69723, 49887, 43463, 19909, ?

Test 42

Fill in the blanks to make two words
that are synonyms. The words spiral
around the circle, one reading clockwise,
the other reading counterclockwise.

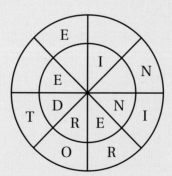

Test 43

Rearrange the letters in the
words below to spell out three colors.

LOW ON BEANBURGER

Test 44

What three-letter word can follow
the first word and precede the second
to make two new words or phrases?

IMP, OR

Test 45

NEAT SQUIRE is an anagram
of what 10-letter word?

Test 46

Which two words below are opposite in meaning?

NAÏVE, HOPEFUL, SLY, BRAVE, SILLY, OPEN

Test 47

Which of the five boxes below has
the most in common with the box above?

A   B   C   D   E

Test 48

What does LOGICAL mean?

STRAIGHT, RATIONAL, CORRECT,
PLAIN, or STRATEGIC

Test 49

Which two words below
are opposite in meaning?

MAGICAL, DISMAL, SAGACIOUS,
FOOLISH, PONDEROUS, GENEROUS

Test 50

What two words that sound alike
but are spelled differently mean
CHANGE and COMMUNION TABLE?

Test 51

Which is the odd one out?

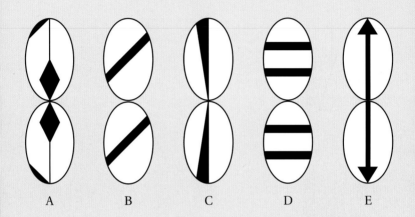

A   B   C   D   E

Test 52

Which of the following is not an anagram of a gem?

RIZNOC, MODNAID, NIZNAI,
PIREHPSA, or THINCAJ

Test 53

What number should logically
replace the question mark?

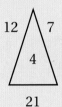 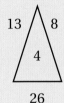 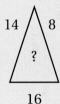

Test 54

Which word below is most likely
to appear in a dictionary definition of EPOXY?

OXYGEN, GOLD, SILVER,
BRONZE, or PLATINUM

Test 55

What does HALBERD mean?

DRAGON, FISH, WEAPON, BIRD, or FLOWER

Test 56

Which is the odd one out?

RUGBY, CRICKET, SOCCER,
BASKETBALL, SWIMMING, TENNIS

Test 57

Insert the letters below left into the blank
spaces to create two words that are synonyms.

ECLLMNNRTU   _ A G _ _ _ I _   A _ _ _ _ I _ G

Test 58

What number should logically
replace the question mark?

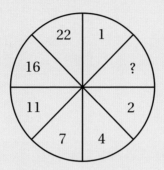

Test 59

EMERALD : GREEN ::

A. TOPAZ : BLACK
B. JASPER : RED
C. OPAL : ORANGE
D. SAPPHIRE : BLUE
E. GARNET : YELLOW

Test 60

Each of the nine squares in the grid marked
from 1A to 3C should incorporate all of the lines and
symbols that are in the squares of the same letter
and number at the top and on the left.

For example, 3B should incorporate all the
lines and symbols that are in boxes 3 and B.

Which one square is incorrect?

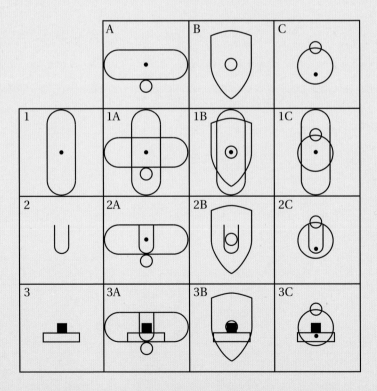

Test 61

4839 : 5748 : 6657

Which numbers below have the same
relationship to one another as the numbers above?

A. 7392 : 8273 : 9182
B. 4915 : 5824 : 6743
C. 9846 : 8827 : 7636
D. 3726 : 4635 : 5544
E. 4829 : 5738 : 7647

Test 62

SENATE, PANAMA, DOSAGE, CURATE, BEFORE

Which word below logically
belongs with the words above?

SIERRA, VOLUME, WAITER, SICKLE, or RHYTHM

Test 63

Which two words below are closest in meaning?

PERFORM, COUNCIL, RECKON,
CONCLAVE, ENDOW, MIRROR

Test 64

Change one letter in each word of
SIN ON O NUN to make a well-known phrase.

Test 65

What letter should logically
replace the question mark?

A	C	F
D	?	I
H	J	M

Test 66

Rearrange the letters in the words
below to spell out three dances.

BOWL MUG AT TARZAN

Test 67

Fill in the blanks to make two words
that are synonyms. The words spiral
around the circle, one reading clockwise,
the other reading counterclockwise.

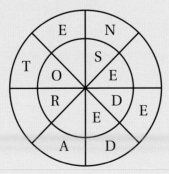

Test 68

ENGINE : CABOOSE ::

A. BOOK : SPINE
B. MERCURY : VENUS
C. MARCH : MAY
D. ALPHA : OMEGA
E. FOLLOW : CONTINUE

Test 69

Which is the odd one out?

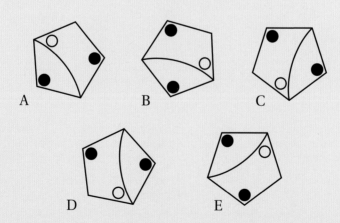

Test 70

Which of the following is not an anagram of a cloud?

RUCSIR, STARSALTOUT, ADORNTO,
LUSUMUC, or SUBMIN

Test 71

Which is the odd one out?

PITTANCE, HEIST, FELONY,
MISDEMEANOR, COUNTERFEITING

Test 72

Which word below means a group of STUDENTS?

HARRAS, FRATERNITY,
PLETHORA, or HILL

Test 73

Which word below is most likely
to appear in a dictionary definition of NEGUS?

WINE, MEDICINE, MILK, LICORICE, or AMBER

Test 74

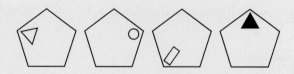

What continues the above sequence?

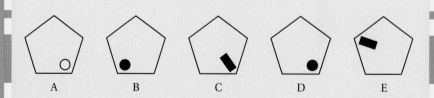

Test 75

What does MAZARINE mean?

ORANGE, DEEP BLUE,
GRAY, BROWN, or SILVERY PINK

Test 76

What number should logically
replace the question mark?

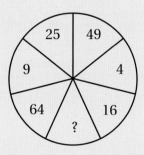

Test 77

A farmer has 200 yards of fencing and wishes to enclose a rectangular area of the greatest possible size.

How big will the area be?

A. 400 sq. yd.
B. 1000 sq. yd.
C. 2000 sq. yd.
D. 2500 sq. yd.
E. 4000 sq. yd.

Test 78

What three-letter word can follow
the first word and precede the second
to make two new words or phrases?

STAND, HAND

Test 79

Which two words below are opposite in meaning?

INFERNAL, COMMODIOUS, CRAMPED,
GLORIOUS, DECOMPOSED, MAGNANIMOUS

Test 80

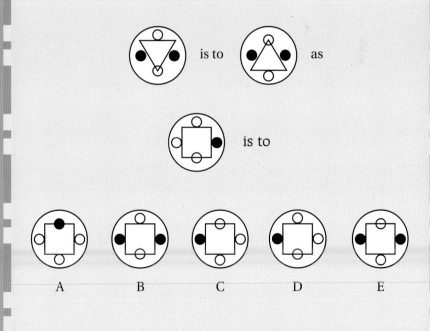

A   B   C   D   E

Test 81

Fill in the blanks to make two words
that are synonyms. The words spiral
around the circle, one reading clockwise,
the other reading counterclockwise.

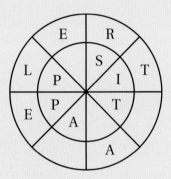

Test 82

Insert the letters below left into the blank
spaces to create two words that are antonyms.

BBEFLORSUX   _ T _ _ B _ _ N   _ L _ _ I _ _ E

Test 83

What number should logically
replace the question mark?

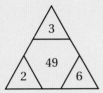 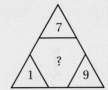

Test 84

Which is the odd one out?

A. $\frac{75}{15} \times 12$

B. $84 \times \frac{7}{3} \times \frac{3}{4}$

C. $78 \times \frac{2}{4} \times 3 - (11 \times \sqrt{25})$

D. $(3^3 \times 2) + \sqrt{36}$

E. $(80\% \times 90) \times 2 + \sqrt{9}$

Test 85

Which two words below are opposite in meaning?

CONTEMPT, INCOMPETENT, RESTFUL,
SINGULAR, INANE, ADEQUATE

Test 86

What continues the above sequence?

A   B   C   D   E

Test 87

Which two words below are opposite in meaning?

POSTPONE, COLLECT, ADVANCE,
ADHERE, CHANGE, APPLY

Test 88

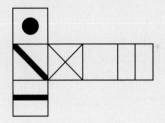

When the above is folded to form a cube,
which one of the following can be produced?

| A | B | C | D | E |

Test 89

SILK : GOSSAMER ::

A. LINEN : CHIFFON
B. COTTON : TAFFETA
C. JUTE : MUSLIN
D. LATIN : ACRYLIC
E. WOOL : ANGORA

Test 90

There are just seven letters that only appear exactly once in the grid.

What U.S. geographical and biographical name can they be arranged to spell out?

L	V	C	G	T	Y	Q	J
F	I	U	P	G	A	W	F
Z	C	Y	R	K	E	H	S
H	O	J	W	Z	N	B	L
F	X	M	Q	G	P	V	U
T	B	E	K	X	R	D	C

Test 91

What does INTAGLIO mean?

HAREM, RESTAURANT, CUT FIGURE,
NARROW BOAT, or PICTURE

Test 92

Which is the odd one out?

GRIDDLE, MICROWAVE, OVEN,
REREDOS, ROTISSERIE, GRILL

Test 93

What does EPOCH mean?

TIME FOR CELEBRATION, MEMORABLE DATE,
HOLIDAY, REST, or BANQUET

Test 94

What number should logically
replace the question mark?

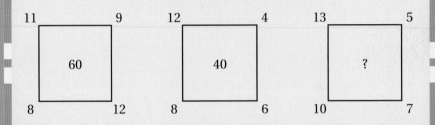

Test 95

RIOTING OAR is an anagram
of what 10-letter word?

Test 96

What three-letter word can follow
the first word and precede the second to
make two new words or phrases?

SADDLE, LADY

Test 97

$3 - (7 + 5) - 2 \times 6 = ?$

Test 98

Combine two of the three-letter
bits below to make a monster.

GIA, LOG, GON, RES, NUT, DRA

Test 99

What two words that sound
alike but are spelled differently
mean THRASH and VEGETABLE?

Test 100

Which circle should logically
replace the question mark?

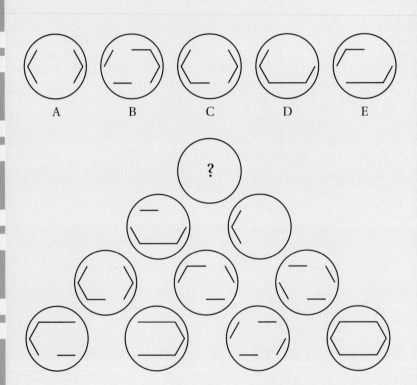

Test 101

What three-letter word
can precede all of the following
words to make new words?

TIES, TRY, ACHE

Test 102

What word that means UNIVERSAL
becomes a word meaning HUMOROUS
when a letter is removed?

Test 103

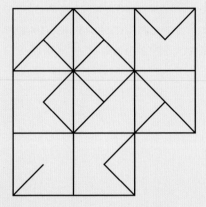

Which square below logically belongs
in the lower right space above?

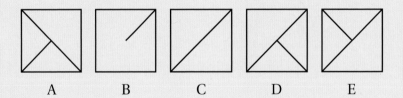

A   B   C   D   E

Test 104

Fill in the blanks to make two words that are antonyms. The words spiral around the circle, one reading clockwise, the other reading counterclockwise.

Test 105

What number should logically replace the question mark?

7		11		17
23		36		?
71		111		169

Test 106

RENT DEBATE is an anagram
of what female given name?

Test 107

Which two words below are closest in meaning?

DIP, SATURATE, DRAIN, DOUSE, STAIN, CLOY

Test 108

Fill in the blanks, one letter per blank,
to create a common word.

_ _ _ W A W A _

Test 109

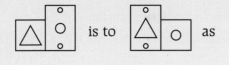

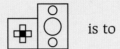

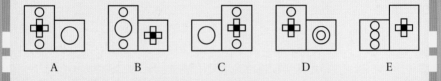

A   B   C   D   E

Test 110

What six-letter word has STRAIGHTFORWARD
and COMMAND as meanings?

Test 111

What does KIBITZER mean?

MEAL, PORTRAIT, DRINK, REFUGE, or ONLOOKER

Test 112

What two words that sound alike but are spelled differently mean MODEST and PURSUED?

Test 113

Which is the odd one out?

POEM, PERSIMMON, HEPTASTICH, VERSE, QUATRAIN

Test 114

What number should logically replace the question mark?

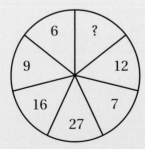

Test 115

How many different teams of five people
can be made from nine people?

Test 116

Which two words below are opposite in meaning?

MANLY, DEXTERITY, RESPECTFUL,
CLUMSINESS, INCOGNITO, WATCHFUL

Test 117

What phrase is represented by the following?
Hint: New attitude

EARTH

Test 118

Which of the following is
not an anagram of a tree?

RAPPOL, LOWLIW, LOWLIP,
CHARL, or REDOAD

Test 119

6589 : 1414 : 28

Which numbers below have the same
relationship to one another as the numbers above?

A. 4839 : 2161 : 14
B. 7836 : 1590 : 69
C. 8526 : 1470 : 1011
D. 9909 : 5112 : 76
E. 3798 : 1215 : 27

Test 120

Each line and symbol that appears in the
four outer circles above is transferred to
the center circle according to these rules:

If the line or symbol occurs in the outer circles
one time, it is transferred,
two times, it is possibly transferred,
three times, it is transferred, and
four times, it is not transferred.

Which of the circles below should appear
at the center of the diagram?

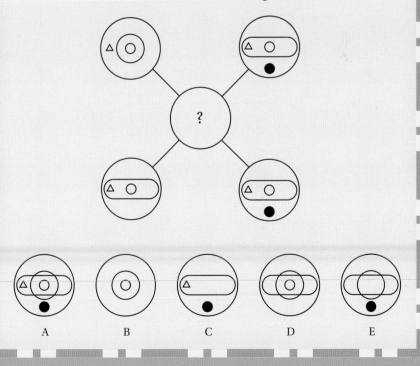

A   B   C   D   E

Test 121

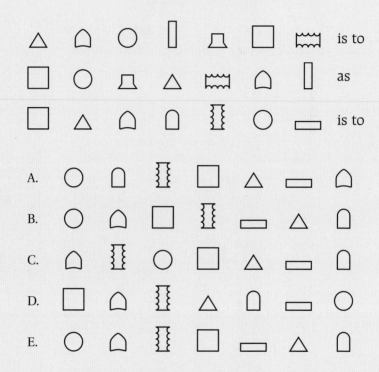

Test 122

What two words that sound alike
but are spelled differently mean

VERGE and GROANED?

Test 123

Which word below is most likely to appear
in a dictionary definition of BUCKRAM?

LINEN, GLASS, COPPER, LACE, or WOOL

Test 124

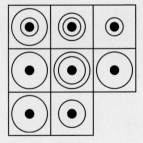

Which square below logically belongs
in the lower right space above?

A   B   C   D   E

Test 125

What does FRANCHISE mean?

FRENCH FOOD, LICENSE TO MARKET,
ABILITY, DEVOTION, or HATRED

Test 126

What four-letter word can follow the first word and
precede the second to make two new words or phrases?

PATCH, WEEK

Test 127

BERRY, COST, KNOT, HINT

Which word below logically
belongs with the words above?

FORD, DIRT, WAGE, PARTY, or SHY

Test 128

Start at any letter and move from
square to square horizontally or vertically,
but not diagonally, to spell out a 12-letter word.
You must provide the missing letters.

I		T
D	E	E
I		R
N	T	E

Test 129

What number should logically
replace the question mark?

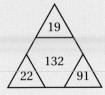
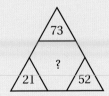

Test 130

What letter is two to the right of the letter that is four to the left of the letter that is immediately to the right of the letter that is three to the left of the letter H?

A B C D E F G H

Test 131

Take one letter, in order, from each of the antonyms of SEVERE given below to form another antonym.

TRACTABLE, GENIAL, EASY, MANAGEABLE, GENTLE, COMPASSIONATE, LENIENT

Test 132

What number should logically replace the question mark?

Test 133

The letters below represent a phrase where the initial letters of each word and the spaces have been removed. What is the phrase?

POATE

Test 134

Which two words below are opposite in meaning?

PENITENT, ASTRINGENT, SALUBRIOUS, SEPARATING, PURPOSEFUL, TRIUMPHANT

Test 135

What five-letter word has BANTER and HUSKS as meanings?

Test 136

Which is the odd one out?

ICOSAHEDRON, PRISM, CYLINDER,
HEXAGON, DODECAHEDRON

Test 137

Fill in the blanks to make two words
that are synonyms. The words spiral
around the circle, one reading clockwise,
the other reading counterclockwise.

Test 138

Combine two of the three-letter
bits below to make a wrestling hold.

HEA, ARM, LOK, SON, LOC, NEL

Test 139

Which two words below
are closest in meaning?

CIRRUS, PENINSULAR, COL,
SAND BAR, DEPRESSION, MISTRAL

Test 140

Each of the nine squares in the grid marked
from 1A to 3C should incorporate all of the lines
and symbols that are in the squares of the same
letter and number at the top and on the left.
For example, 3B should incorporate all the lines
and symbols that are in boxes 3 and B.

Which one square is incorrect?

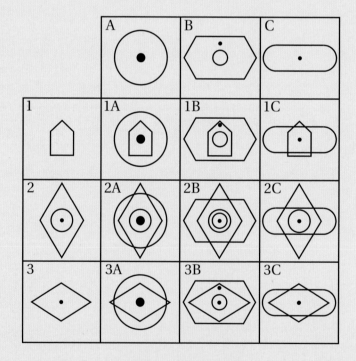

Test 141

Fill in the blanks to make two words that
are synonyms. The words spiral around
the circle, one reading clockwise,
the other reading counterclockwise.

Test 142

What number should logically
replace the question mark?

237 : 4280 : 582
863 : 14424 : 416
523 : ? : 826

Test 143

Which of the following is not
an anagram of a composer?

A. SCI SOAP
B. IS IRONS
C. COLD PAN
D. WE RANG
E. MR. HALE

Test 144

Which of the five boxes below has
the most in common with the box above?

A   B   C   D   E

Test 145

What numbers should logically
replace the question marks?

3	6	?	330
2	5	?	41

Test 146

Insert the correct pair of words into
the blank spaces in the sentence below.

The problem with the use of ___ is that
they are often only ___ by the person using them.

    A. COMPUTERS, ACCESSED
    B. ABBREVIATIONS, UNDERSTOOD
    C. ANAGRAMS, TRANSLATED
    D. WORDS, SPOKEN
    E. EPITAPHS, APPRECIATED

Test 147

RUDE TAVERN is an anagram
of what 10-letter word?

Test 148

Which number is the odd one out?

67626, 84129, 36119, 25622, 32418

Test 149

Which two words below are closest in meaning?

LIBERTINE, EPHEMERAL, BRIEF,
PLACID, IMMORTAL, PRECISE

Test 150

Which is the odd one out?

DOE, JENNY, COB, EWE, SOW

Test 151

What two words that sound alike
but are spelled differently mean
SASH and COMBINATION OF NOTES?

Test 152

What seven-letter word has DIVISION OF BOOK
and RELIGIOUS MEETING as meanings?

Test 153

What number should logically
replace the question mark?

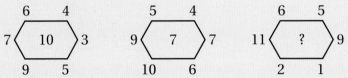

Test 154

Which word below is most likely to appear
in a dictionary definition of BISQUE?

BISCUITS, CUSTARD, PLUMS, CHICKEN, or SOUP

Test 155

Which two words below
are opposite in meaning?

POPULATED, DIMINUTIVE, DEVOTION,
GARGANTUAN, DEVOID, SUCCESSFUL

Test 156

Combine two of the three-letter
bits below to make a dance.

TOT, TEZ, ANE, WAL, PAV, FOX

Test 157

$$\frac{3 + 6 \times 2}{3 + 2 \times 3} = ?$$

Test 158

What does KELP mean?

DRINK, SWOLLEN FEET, SEAWEED,
SCAR, or MUSICAL PIECE

Test 159

Which is the odd one out?

PEPPERONI, SAUSAGE, SAUERKRAUT,
CHIPOLATA, KNACKWURST

Test 160

Which circle should logically
replace the question mark?

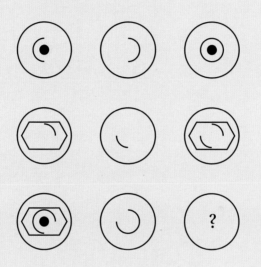

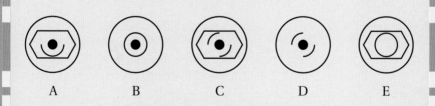

A B C D E

Test 161

Which is the odd one out?

A   B   C   D   E

Test 162

TRIANGLE : HEXAGON ::

A. SQUARE : PENTAGON
B. PENTAGON : HEPTAGON
C. HEXAGON : OCTAGON
D. SQUARE : OCTAGON
E. CIRCLE : PENTAGON

Test 163

What is the result of multiplying the sum of
the odd numbers in the left-hand grid by the sum
of the even numbers in the right-hand grid?

28	16	5	36
22	6	2	4
9	18	3	42
17	1	6	15

4	37	10	1
3	2	15	7
14	17	19	9
5	32	23	8

Test 164

FAME, BID, POUND, LAND, REMIT

Which word below logically continues
the sequence of words above?

CREST, BOUND, GRUNT, CHARGE, or FLOAT

Test 165

What continues the above sequence?

A   B   C   D   E

Test 166

What number should logically replace the question mark?

6	8	12
10	2	5
15	4	?

Test 167

ACCORD TIME is an anagram
of what 10-letter word?

Test 168

Which word below is an
antonym of INTELLIGIBLE?

PROFLIGATE, LUCID, STUPID,
PLAIN, or CONFUSED

Test 169

Change one letter in each word of
COME GAS LOT GUILT AN I PAY
to make a well-known phrase.

Test 170

What four-letter word has REMAINDER
and REPOSE as meanings?

Test 171

What does FRISSON mean?

CANNON, THUNDERBOLT, CREVICE,
THRILL, or ESCARPMENT

Test 172

What number should logically
replace the question mark?

26, −39, 58$^1/_2$, −87$^3/_4$, ?

Test 173

What six-letter word can follow the
first word and precede the second to
make two new words or phrases?

POST, CHEF

Test 174

What number should logically replace the question mark?

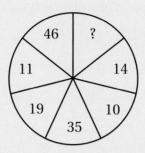

Test 175

Which two words below are closest in meaning?

PAWNBROKER, DRAGOMAN, CHARLATAN,
TRADER, ARTIST, INTERPRETER

Test 176

What two words that sound alike but are
spelled differently mean TREE and SHORE?

Test 177

Which is the odd one out?

TANKER, CLIPPER, GALLEON,
SLOOP, CARAVEL

Test 178

What four-letter word has GOSSIP
and BIRD as meanings?

Test 179

Which of the following is
not an anagram of a flower?

ADFFODLI, PULTI, LIDLAIOG,
TUBERT, or NASPY

Test 180

Which circle should logically
replace the question mark?

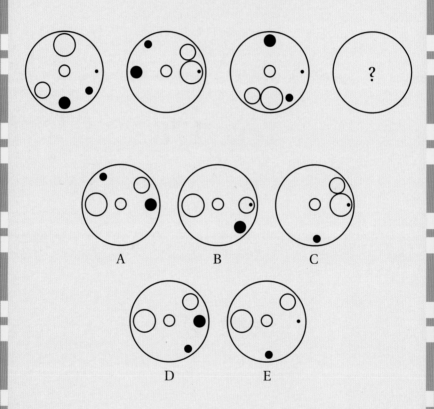

Test 181

Which is the odd one out?

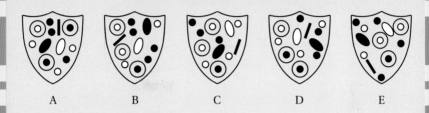

A   B   C   D   E

Test 182

Fill in the blanks to make two words
that are antonyms. The words spiral
around the circle, one reading clockwise,
the other reading counterclockwise.

Test 183

What number should logically
replace the question mark?

14, 91, 62, 53, 64, ?

A. 78
B. 96
C. 98
D. 68
E. 44

Test 184

GET SOUSING is an anagram
of what 10-letter word?

Test 185

Which word below is an antonym of OPTIMUM?

GLUM, MINIMAL, MANDATORY,
DISTANT, or CLOSE

Test 186

What continues the above sequence?

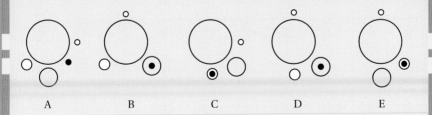

A   B   C   D   E

Test 187

SEISMOLOGY : EARTHQUAKES ::

A. CARPOLOGY : MAPS
B. DENDROLOGY : WIND
C. OROLOGY : MOUNTAINS
D. DELTIOLOGY : ROCKS
E. TOPOGRAPHY : CAVES

Test 188

Starting at one of the corner squares,
what nine-letter word can be formed
by spiraling clockwise around the perimeter
and finishing at the center square.
(You must provide the missing letters.)

E	R	
		H
O	L	E

Test 189

What letter should logically
replace the question mark?

A, D, F, I, K, ?

Test 190

What two words that sound alike but are
spelled differently mean FABRICATE and INVOICED?

Test 191

What four-letter word has STEEL
INSTRUMENT and FOLDER as meanings?

Test 192

What number should logically
replace the question mark?

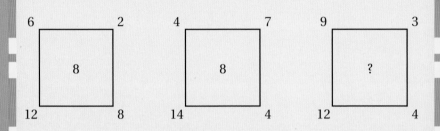

6   2   4   7   9   3

8   8   ?

12   8   14   4   12   4

Test 193

Which is the odd one out?

TYPHOON, FAVEOLATE, HURRICANE,
MISTRAL, PAMPERO

Test 194

Which two words below are opposite in meaning?

LANCINATE, THOUGHTFUL,
DEMONIC, CONSIDERATE, MEND

Test 195

Which of the following is not an anagram of a vegetable?

TATOOP, BAGCABE, OUTSPRS,
GENORA, RORCAT

Test 196

What eight-letter musical instrument can be put in the boxes to make three-letters words reading down?

P	F	A	L	O	H	O	M
A	L	L	A	B	E	W	A

Test 197

Three coins are tossed in the air at the same time. What are the chances that at least two of the coins will finish heads up?

Test 198

What does JENNY mean?

YOUNG DEER, STAMP, FEMALE DONKEY, BRIDGE SUPPORT, or STOAT

Test 199

What four-letter word can follow the first word and precede the second to make two new words or phrases?

CAST, FILINGS

Test 200

Which circle should logically
replace the question mark?

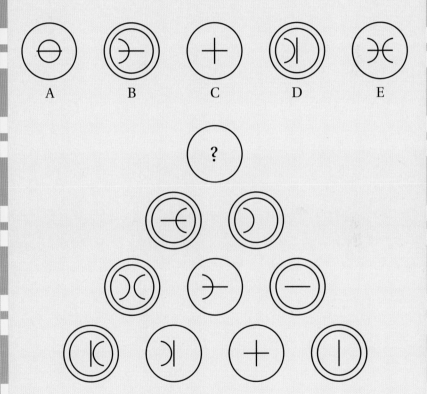

Test 201

What number should logically
replace the question mark?

15		17
	3	
8		12

54		74
	4	
14		39

21		89
	?	
56		18

Test 202

What six-letter creature can be put in the boxes
to make three-letter words reading down?

L	D	M	A	P	H
O	U	A	S	I	E

Test 203

Which is the odd one out?

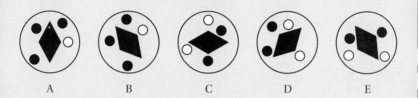

A   B   C   D   E

Test 204

Which two words below are closest in meaning?

INCIDENTAL, INVASIVE, INAUGURAL,
INTRINSIC, BOLD, NATIVE

Test 205

Which is the odd one out?

APRIL, SEPTEMBER, NOVEMBER, AUGUST, JUNE

Test 206

LARBOARD : SHIP :: VERSO :

A. POEM
B. CAR
C. TRUNK
D. PORT
E. BOOK

Test 207

What number should logically replace the question mark?

4	5	9	4	2
8	6	2	6	4
2	3	?	2	7
7	1	2	3	5
3	8	3	6	2

Test 208

Fill in the blanks with a part of the human body,
one letter per blank, to create a common word.

C A _ _ _ E R

Test 209

What continues the above sequence?

A   B   C   D   E

Test 210

POLICE SECT is an anagram
of what 10-letter word?

Test 211

A man has four socks in his drawer.
Each sock is either black or white.
The chances of him selecting a pair at
random and finding that he has a white pair is 0.5.
What are his chances of the pair being black?

Test 212

Which of the following is
not an anagram of a boat?

LEVACAR, ONCAE, CHUNAL,
RUTCK, or ERSCRUI

Test 213

What does MOLLIFY mean?

TRANSFORM, CHANGE, APPEASE,
ENJOIN, or SOLIDIFY

Test 214

What four-letter word has
FERMENTED LIQUOR and LEA as meanings?

Test 215

What does KOOKABURRA mean?

KINGFISHER, NATIVE OF GUINEA,
DINGHY, WATERFALL, or HUT

Test 216

What four-letter word can precede all of
the following words to make new words?

BALL, MAIDEN, SOME, CART, BILL

Test 217

Combine two of the three-letter bits
below to make another name for Japan.

PON, EAS, PAM, NIP, ISL, JAN

Test 218

Fill in the blanks to make two words that are synonyms. The words spiral around the circle, one reading clockwise, the other reading counterclockwise.

Test 219

Which word below is most likely to appear in a dictionary definition of GALANTINE?

LARD, PASTA, VINEGAR, BREAD, or MEAT

Test 220

Each line and symbol that appears in the
four outer circles below is transferred to
the center circle according to these rules:

If the line or symbol occurs in the outer circles
one time, it is transferred,
two times, it is possibly transferred,
three times, it is transferred, and
four times, it is not transferred.

Which of the circles below should appear
at the center of the diagram?

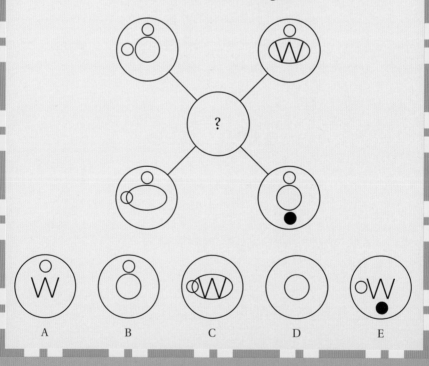

Test 221

Which four of the five figures below
can be joined together to form a perfect square?

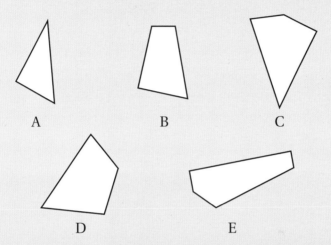

A

B

C

D

E

Test 222

FLEW POLISH is an anagram
of what 10-letter word?

Test 223

97318462 : 86719243 :: 43967512 :

A. 13675942
B. 71364259
C. 71346295
D. 17634259
E. 71364529

Test 224

Which of the following is not
an anagram of a musical instrument?

ON CERT, AS BOSON, LIP COCO,
ARTISAN, or ACID CROON

Test 225

Which two words below are opposite in meaning?

SLANT, PLETHORA, PREDICAMENT,
PLIGHT, DEARTH, AIGRETTE

Test 226

Which is the odd one out?

A   B   C   D   E

Test 227

What number should logically
replace the question mark?

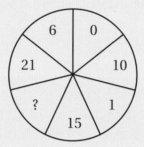

Test 228

What does SUPPLANT mean?

PLIANT, FIX, OUST, AUGMENT, or SUSTAIN

Test 229

Change one letter in each
word of DON'S MAKE CHANGES
to make a well-known phrase.

Test 230

Fill in the blanks to make two words
that are synonyms. The words spiral
around the circle, one reading clockwise,
the other reading counterclockwise.

Test 231

What number should logically
replace the question mark?

12, 33, 66, 132, 363, ?

Test 232

What word is represented by the following?
Hint: Pure

Test 233

Which is the odd one out?

GASKIN, STIFLE, HOCK,
FETLOCK, GIBUS

Test 234

What does FORAY mean?

RETREAT, REBEL, SHIRK,
PILLAGE, or MAGNIFY

Test 235

Which word below is most likely
to appear in a dictionary definition of PONGEE?

GABARDINE, SILK, TWEED, LACE, or LEATHER

Test 236

What four-letter word can precede
all of the following words to make new words?
FALL, MILL, WARD, SWEPT, BREAKER

Test 237

Which of the following is not
an anagram of a form of transportation?

INATR, BINMOUS, LECYC, MART, or RUGAS

Test 238

What does CHICANERY mean?

TORTUOUS, BOASTFULNESS,
OPPORTUNISM, TRICKERY, or VISION

Test 239

What four-letter word has PARASITE
and MATTRESS COVER as meanings?

Test 240

Each line and symbol that appears in the
four outer circles below is transferred to
the center circle according to these rules:

If the line or symbol occurs in the outer circles
one time, it is transferred,
two times, it is possibly transferred,
three times, it is transferred, and
four times, it is not transferred.

Which of the circles below should appear
at the center of the diagram?

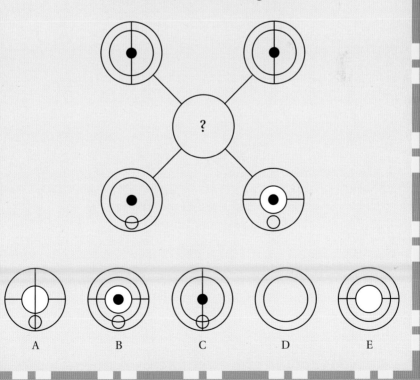

Test 241

Fill in the blanks to make two words
that are synonyms. The words spiral
around the circle, one reading clockwise,
the other reading counterclockwise.

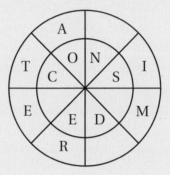

Test 242

HOTEL NOOSE is an anagram
of what well-known phrase?
Hint: Fugitive

Test 243

3469 : 3515 : 3566

Which numbers below have the same
relationship to one another as the numbers above?

A. 5783 : 5861 : 5947
B. 7842 : 7914 : 8361
C. 4821 : 4842 : 4884
D . 9817 : 9899 : 9967
E. 1236 : 1248 : 1260

Test 244

Take one letter, in order, from each
of the synonyms of COMPETENT
given below to form another synonym.

APPROPRIATE, CLEVER, DEXTROUS,
FIT, QUALIFIED, SUFFICIENT, PRACTICED,
ABLE, ENDOWED, SUITABLE

Test 245

What four-letter word has SLIDE
and UNDERWEAR as meanings?

Test 246

Which is the odd one out?

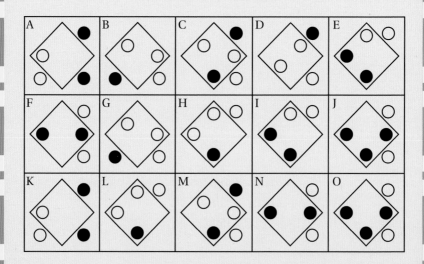

Test 247

What four-letter word can follow the first word and precede the second to make two new words or phrases?

SO, RATE

Test 248

What does LATENT mean?

WORTHY, VEILED, LATTERLY, FLANKING, or EVIDENT

Test 249

Which is the odd one out?

ETHER, VACUUM, WELKIN, NEOPHYTE, SKY

Test 250

On Digital Avenue, houses are numbered consecutively, starting at 1. There is only one house on the street that has a house number where the sum of the digits is exactly twice the product of the digits. What is that number, and what is the greatest number of houses that there could be on Digital Avenue?

Test 251

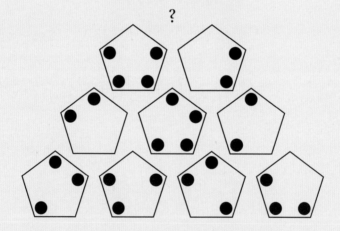

Which pentagon should logically replace the question mark?

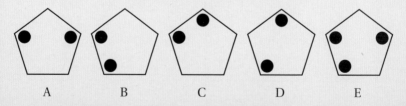

| A | B | C | D | E |

Test 252

What number should logically
replace the question mark?

5	7	6	8
6	2	5	1
?	4	9	5
3	5	2	4

Test 253

What does PALFREY mean?

BIRD, REPTILE, INSECT, FISH, or HORSE

Test 254

Which two words below are closest in meaning?

CRISTATE, CROSSED, MORIBUND,
ELEVATED, TUFTED, CRYSTALLIZED

Test 255

What two words that sound alike but are spelled
differently mean BARTER and SMALL ROOM?

Test 256

Which of the following is not an anagram of a fish?

WALLSOW, TRUBTO, DERFOULN,
CAPLIE, or DAHDCKO

Test 257

What does CORDATE mean?

HEART-SHAPED, PEAR-SHAPED,
LEMON-SHAPED, CYLINDRICAL, or DYNAMIC

Test 258

Combine two of the three-letter bits
below to make a word meaning mud.

DGE, MIR, SWA, MPE, ESE, SLU

Test 259

What three-letter word can precede all
of the following words to make new words?

DATE, DRILL, DRAKE, KIND, GO

Test 260

Which circle should logically
replace the question mark?

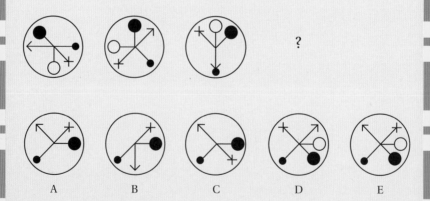

A   B   C   D   E

Test 261

What continues the above sequence?

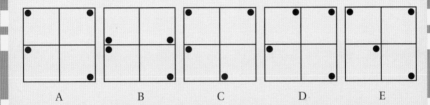

A   B   C   D   E

Test 262

Rearrange the letters in the words
below to spell out three cities.

WHAT PASSIONATE ART

Test 263

What number should logically
replace the question mark?

48725, 5274, 425, ?

Test 264

Which word below is
an antonym of SUPERB?

HUMBLE, OLD, PATHETIC,
WORN, or CHEAP

Test 265

Which two words below are closest in meaning?

PROFANITY, CARE, ABUSE,
WISDOM, GAIN, THOUGHT

Test 266

What number should logically
replace the question mark?

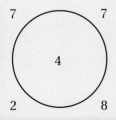
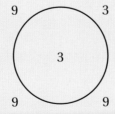
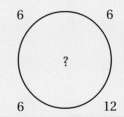

Test 267

Which is the odd one out?

ELABORATE, EXPOUND, ENLARGE,
EXTEMPORIZE, EXPATIATE

Test 268

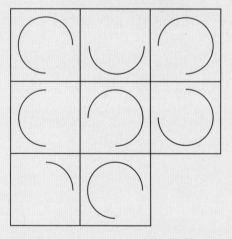

Which square below logically belongs
in the lower right space above?

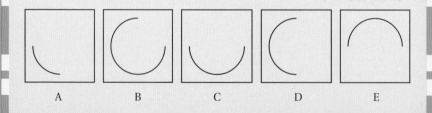

A   B   C   D   E

Test 269

What is the probability of selecting
a face card (jack, queen, or king) at random
from a standard deck of 52 cards?

Test 270

FISCAL SIDE is an anagram
of what 10-letter word?

Test 271

What number should logically
replace the question mark?

26, 34, 41, 46, 56, ?

Test 272

What does QUINNAT mean?

HEADDRESS, CUCUMBER, REINDEER,
KING SALMON, or WEAPON

Test 273

What three-letter word
can precede all of the following
words to make new words?

SCRIPT, TENT, VERSE,
JUNCTION, TEST

Test 274

Which is the odd one out?

FLORET, LUCARNE,
DORMER, ORIEL, CASEMENT

Test 275

Which two words below
are closest in meaning?

BALEFUL, PROBLEMATIC, PERNICIOUS,
NOXIOUS, RESIDUAL, PHLEGMATIC

Test 276

Fill in the blanks to make two words that are synonyms.
The words spiral around the circle, one reading
clockwise, the other reading counterclockwise.

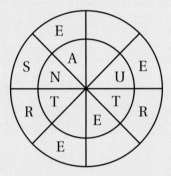

Test 277

Which of the following is not an anagram of an animal?

RANBYD, RITEG, PALEDOR, FABFULO, or KONDYE

Test 278

What eight-letter word has SIGNIFY
and CONFIDENTIAL as meanings?

Test 279

What does HYPERBOLE mean?

POETIC, ANGELIC, NONSENSICAL,
EXAGGERATION, or IMAGINATION

Test 280

Which is the odd one out?

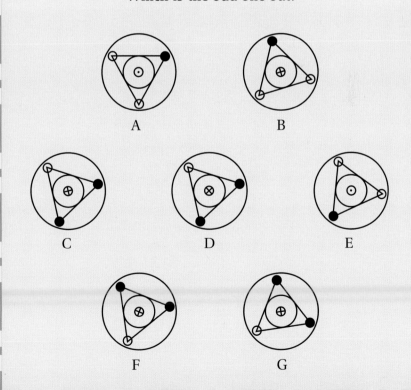

A

B

C

D

E

F

G

Test 281

Fill in the blanks to make two words
that are antonyms. The words spiral
around the circle, one reading clockwise,
the other reading counterclockwise.

Test 282

BOLD ALICIA is an anagram
of what 10-letter word?

Test 283

What number should logically
replace the question mark?

 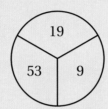 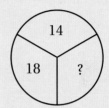

Test 284

What two words that differ by one
letter mean CHANNEL OR PIPE and DIRECT?

Test 285

Which is the odd one out?

TANGENT, DIAMETER,
CHORD, HYPOTENUSE, SECANT

Test 286

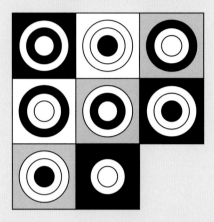

Which square below logically
belongs in the lower right space above?

A   B   C   D   E

Test 287

If the black dot moves two corners counterclockwise
at each stage, and the white dot moves three corners
clockwise at each stage, in how many stages
will they be together in the same corner?

Test 288

Which two words below are closest in meaning?

LIAISON, AEGIS, ADVICE,
HOPE, AFFECTION, PATRONAGE

Test 289

If you write down my age followed by my age when
I was a year younger, you get a four-digit number.
Taking the square root of that number gives
my house number. What is it?

Test 290

Start at any letter and move from
square to square horizontally or
vertically, but not diagonally, to
spell out a 12-letter word. You must
provide the missing letters.

	T	I
T	E	T
O	N	S
	E	R

Test 291

Fill in the blanks to make two words
that are synonyms. The words spiral
around the circle, one reading clockwise,
the other reading counterclockwise.

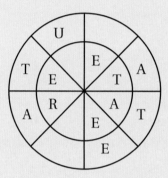

Test 292

What three-letter word can precede
all of the following words to make new words?

GOOSE, DAY, SOON, ARCH, EYED

Test 293

Combine two of the three-letter bits
below to make a child's book.

MOR, CAR, MER, PIC, TON, PRI

Test 294

What number should logically
replace the question mark?

  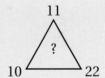

Test 295

Which word below is most likely to appear
in a dictionary definition of BOUILLABAISSE?

BREAD, LEMON, MUSTARD, FISH, or RICE

Test 296

Which of the following is
not an anagram of a bird?

CHIFN, ROWSPAR, BEZAR,
WKAH, or TRUHSH

Test 297

What does CHINCH mean?

BEDBUG, HORSE'S BRIDGE, CEREMONY,
SHORTBEARD, or SHORT MEASURE

Test 298

What six-letter word has NEAT
and TREE as meanings?

Test 299

What number should logically
replace the question mark?

7, 11, 20, ? , 61, 97

Test 300

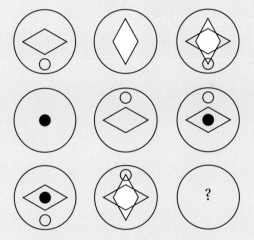

Which circle should logically
replace the question mark?

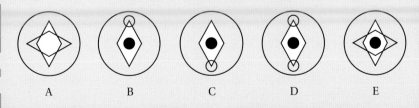

A   B   C   D   E

Brain Stumpers

Stumper 1

Read clockwise to figure out this sixteen-letter word. Only alternate letters are shown, and you have to find the starting point.

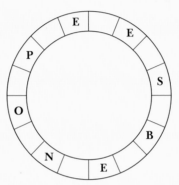

Stumper 2

What number should replace the question mark?

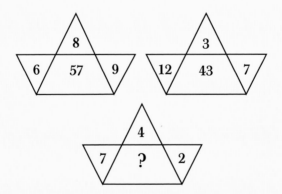

Stumper 3

Only one set of letters below
can be arranged into a five-letter
English word. Can you find the word?

BYRDI	TONET	NRCOL
PUITN	HUTME	LEBIT
TINOL	RUGNE	BEHAD

Stumper 4

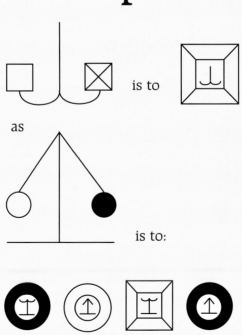

is to

as

is to:

A   B   C   D

Stumper 5

Which three-letter word forms two
other words that are unrelated in meaning
when "LESS" and "NESS" are added to the end?
For example, SOUND: soundless, soundness.
Clue: Foolish deponent

Stumper 6

Which number is the odd one out?

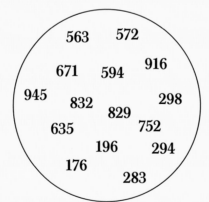

Stumper 7

I create a happy sound on my entire
journey to a place of monetary deposit.

What am I doing?

Stumper 8

Which word comes closest in meaning to mete?

CARRY, ADJOIN, COORDINATE,
ALLOT, PARODY

Stumper 9

Only ten letters of the alphabet do
not appear in this grid. What ten-letter
phrase can they be arranged to spell out?
Clue: Cape Canaveral

P	Z	B	G
M	O	K	J
F	W	Q	X
Y	V	R	D

Stumper 10

What number comes next in this sequence?

483, 759, 264, 837, ?

Stumper 11

What symbol should replace the question mark?

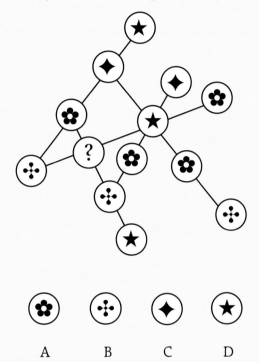

A   B   C   D

Stumper 12

One letter in each word of a well-known saying
has been changed. What is the saying?

TAPE TIE PULL MY TOE CORNS

Stumper 13

What, in connection with this
question, is the next number below?

4, 13, 19, 21, 29, ?

Stumper 14

To what number should the
missing hand on the clock point?

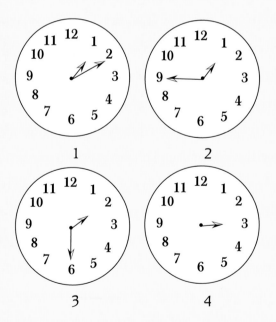

1

2

3

4

Stumper 15

Fill in the blanks with the same seven
letters in the same order so that
the sentence makes complete sense.

A _____ chef was _____

to serve the meal because he had _____.

Stumper 16

LEA : PIE
SAP :

A. BAT
B. WAG
C. BOW
D. WET
E. YET

Stumper 17

What phrase is suggested below?

SH
TT
RG
EN

Stumper 18

What number should appear in
the circle with the question mark?

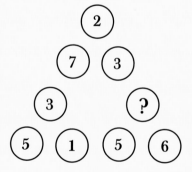

Stumper 19

What face should replace the question mark?

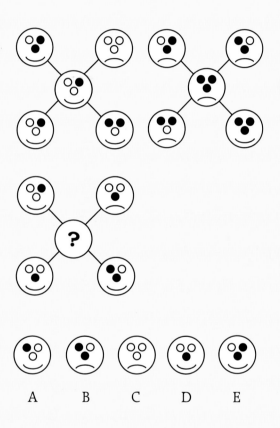

A   B   C   D   E

Stumper 20

Fill in the missing word to complete the crossword.

Stumper 21

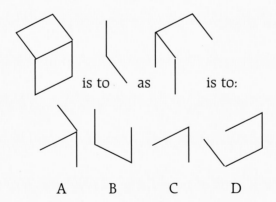

is to ... as ... is to:

A   B   C   D

Stumper 22

EUPHORIA is to BLISS as MELANCHOLY is to:

A. BAWDY
B. UNSEEMLY
C. DESPAIR
D. NEGATE
E. RIBALD

Stumper 23

Which pentagon continues the series?

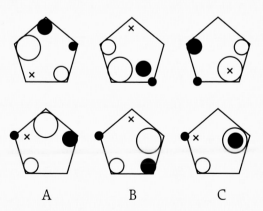

A   B   C

Stumper 24

Place two of the four-letter groups together to make a word.

RIAL - SYCO - TUTO - PANT - PLAT

Stumper 25

Find a one-word anagram in CREAM ELK.

Stumper 26

Simplify $\dfrac{5}{11} \div \dfrac{25}{22}$.

Stumper 27

Trace out a ten-letter word in any
direction, using each letter once only.

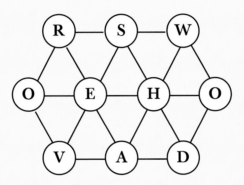

Stumper 28

Simplify $\dfrac{725}{1000}$ as a fraction.

Stumper 29

Which word means the fear of MICE?

A. ANEMOPHOBIA
B. MUSOPHOBIA
C. BAROPHOBIA
D. POTOPHOBIA
E. OCHOPHOBIA

Stumper 30

What is the meaning of PRANDIAL?

A. BREAKFAST
B. TEATIME
C. DINNER
D. SUPPER
E. SNACKS

Stumper 31

A word can be placed inside the parentheses
that has the same meaning as the words outside.
What is it?

TAR (_ _ _ _ _) SET UP

Stumper 32

If 4 × 4 = 20, then 5 × 6 = ?

Stumper 33

Which circle's letters cannot be
rearranged into a six-letter word?

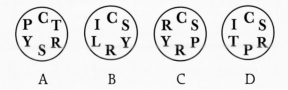

A   B   C   D

Stumper 34

Which number should replace the question mark?

6	8	17	21
13	1	9	10
3	15	4	?
4	6	4	5

Stumper 35

What is the opposite of NEOPHYTE?

A. EARTHLY
B. NOVICE
C. ANCIENT
D. EXPERT
E. STARLIKE

Stumper 36

What number should replace the question mark?

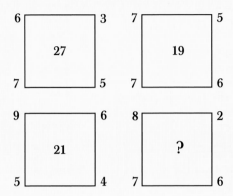

Stumper 37

Which animal does not fit with the others?

A. CHAMOIS
B. TIERCEL
C. IMPALA
D. FENNEC
E. GERBIL
F. JERBOA

Stumper 38

Place the letters in the grid to make a flower and a fish.

G O P P P P U Y Y

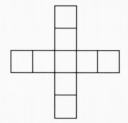

Stumper 39

What is the mathematical sign for "identical with"?

A. [ ]
B. >
C. ≡
D. /
E. <

Stumper 40

Complete the word.

_ _ C K J _ _

Stumper 41

Change SEPTEMBER to JULY.
The asterisks in each word are
common to the word above it.

SEPTEMBER

_ _ _ _ **** _ _   Clue: Hygenic

_ _ * * * _ _ _ _   Clue: Anthropod

_ _ _ * * * _ _   Clue: Numerous

JULY

**

Stumper 42

What number should
replace the question mark?

2	9	7
10	?	12
8	13	5

Stumper 43

The following clue leads to what pair of rhyming words?

SKILLFUL ROBBERY

Stumper 44

Add one letter, not necessarily the same letter, to each word to find eight words that all have something in common.

MAT, SEW, ART, SAG, BAN, FAN, ICE

Stumper 45

Which day is two days before the day after the day three days after the day before Tuesday?

SUNDAY
MONDAY
TUESDAY
WEDNESDAY
THURSDAY
FRIDAY
SATURDAY

Stumper 46

Which of the numbered figures is the odd one out?

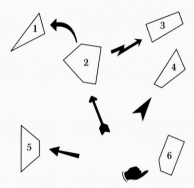

Stumper 47

A pancake can be sliced into four pieces
in any number of ways by using two cuts.
One example is shown to the right.

What is the maximum number of pieces
that can be obtained from a pancake using three cuts?

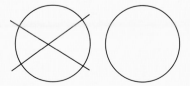

Stumper 48

What well-known proverb is opposite
in meaning to the proverb
"Too many cooks spoil the broth"?

Stumper 49

How many lines appear below?

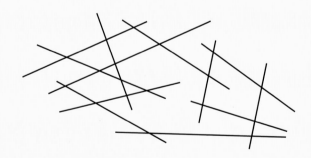

Stumper 50

What number should
replace the question mark?

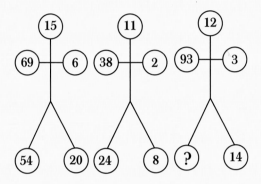

Stumper 51

All widgets are green. Everything green
has a hole in the middle. Some things
that are green have a jagged edge. Therefore:

1. All widgets have a hole in the middle.
2. Everything with a jagged edge is a widget.
3. Neither of the above is true.
4. Both the above are true.

Stumper 52

What number should replace
the question mark?

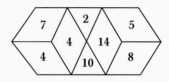

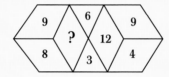

Stumper 53

Unscramble these four anagrammed
words to determine what they have in common.

OGLED, WROTE, CLEATS, PELMET

Stumper 54

Which is the odd one out?

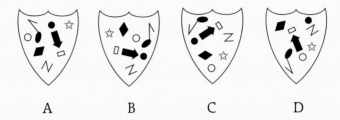

A   B   C   D

Stumper 55

What number should replace
the question mark?

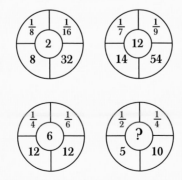

Stumper 56

Rearrange the two five-letter words to form a ten-letter word meaning "trader with Native Americans."

MOOCH CANER

Stumper 57

Which word means the same as VIBRATO?

- A. LUSTROUS
- B. EXCITING
- C. THROBBING
- D. SOFTLY
- E. STATIONARY

Stumper 58

Insert the letters of the phrase FAMILIES MASS SALE into the empty spaces below, using each letter once to complete a palindromic sentence—one that reads the same backwards and forwards.
For example: Madam, I'm Adam.

_ A _ _ _ _ S _ _ _ _ _ _ _ _ S _ _ _

Clue: Relatively altruistic

Stumper 59

"The chance of exposure to the
adverse consequences of future events."

Which word fits closest to the above definition?

A. SPECULATION
B. DANGER
C. RISK
D. WORRY
E. HALLUCINATION

Stumper 60

What number continues this sequence?

8960, 6720, 3360, 840, 630, ?

Stumper 61

What number should replace
the question mark?

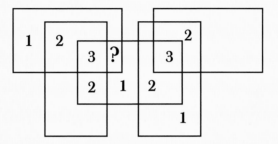

Stumper 62

Which two words below are
closest in meaning?

AUTHENTIC, GERMANE, FOREIGN,
GENTLE, PRODIGIOUS, COGNATE

Stumper 63

Place three of the two-letter groups
together to form a fruit.

OR – LY – AN – EE – GO – CH

Stumper 64

Which is the missing square?

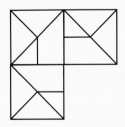

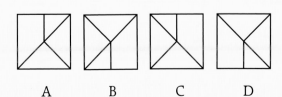

A   B   C   D

Stumper 65

Which word will fit in front of
these words to make new words?

(_ _ _ _)

BOOT
POT
ASS
DAW
HAMMER

Stumper 66

There is a system for pricing the menu.

What would oysters cost?

MENU	
SOUP	$18
SALAD	$23
ROAST BEEF	$41
ICE CREAM	$36
COFFEE	$27

Stumper 67

Which number should replace
the question mark?

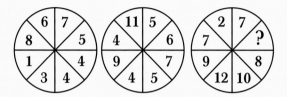

Stumper 68

If the missing letters in the circle below are
correctly inserted, they will form an eight-letter
word. The word will not have to be read in a
clockwise direction, but the letters are consecutive.

What is the word and missing letters?

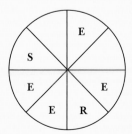

Stumper 69

What is the surface area of this tennis ball?

A. 17.635 sq. in.
B. 18.635 sq. in.
C. 19.635 sq. in.
D. 20.635 sq. in.
E. 21.635 sq. in.

$2^1/_2$in.

Stumper 70

Which of the following is always associated with HAMSTRING?

A. PIGS
B. BACON
C. TENNIS RACQUETS
D. DINNER
E. TENDON

Stumper 71

What number should replace
the question mark?

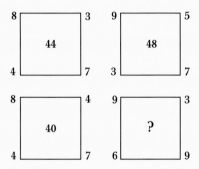

Stumper 72

What number should replace the question mark?

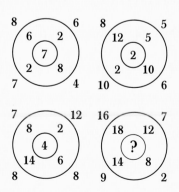

Stumper 73

The vowels have been omitted from this quotation.

Can you replace them?

T S W S F T H R T H T K
N W S H S W N C H L D

Stumper 74

Place the letters in the grid to form
a nautical person and a mineral.

A A C E F I P L O R R R D

Stumper 75

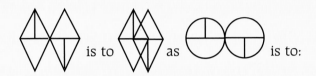 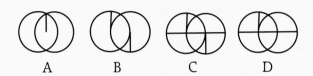

is to ... as ... is to:

A   B   C   D

Stumper 76

Which of the boxes below is
most like the box above?

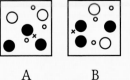

A   B   C   D

Stumper 77

Fill in the missing letters to make a nine-letter word starting from a corner square and spiraling into the center.

U		E
	E	R
E	T	A

Stumper 78

Place two of the four-letter groups together to make a word.

YWAY - ROED -ANAB - ALLE - ALIC - TYPE

Stumper 79

By moving through the doorways,
spell out an eight-letter word.
Each letter may be used only once.

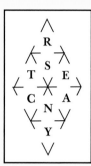

Stumper 80

Fill in the missing letters to make
a nine-letter word starting from a corner
square and continuing in a spiral to the center.

O		E
W	S	R
O	L	

Stumper 81

Complete the word below that contains
a unique trigraph—i.e., three consecutive
letters which appear in no other English word.

_ _ _ _ KSG _ _ _ _ _

Stumper 82

Find just one reason for arranging the
following words into three groups,
each containing three words:

MONKEY, LOANED, CORNER, LONGER, BLONDE,
SPONGE, HORNET, WONDER, BRONZE

Stumper 83

By joining corners and not counting rotations and reflections it is possible to dissect a pentagon into three triangles only one way and a hexagon three different ways. Both are illustrated below:

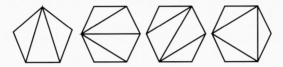

In how many ways is it possible to dissect a heptagon into triangles?

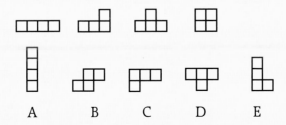

Stumper 84

What completes the below sequence?

A   B   C   D   E

Stumper 85

LARGO : SLOW
PIANO :

A. SMOOTH
B. LOUD
C. SOFT
D. PLAY
E. BRISK

Stumper 86

What number should replace
the question mark?

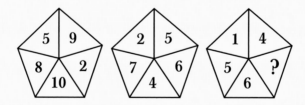

Stumper 87

Tom beats Joe at pool but loses to Sue.
Hilary usually wins against Joe, sometimes
against Tom, but never against Sue.

Who is the weakest player?

Stumper 88

Solve the cryptic clue below. The answer is
a ten-letter anagram contained within the clue:

ESCORT A MAN UNSTEADILY TO
CALIFORNIAN CITY

Stumper 89

Working clockwise, take one letter from each
circle in turn to spell out two synonyms.
Note: Each word starts in a different circle.

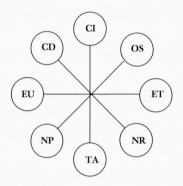

Stumper 90

The die is rolled one face to Square 2, and
so on—one face at a time to Squares 3-4-5-6.

Which number will appear on the top face in Square 6?

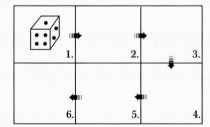

Stumper 91

Which number is the odd one out?

3628, 2426, 4146, 1448

Stumper 92

Insert the numbers 1–5 in the circles, using each number once. Do so in such a way that for any particular circle the sum of the number in the circles connected directly to it add up to the value allocated to the number inside the circle in accordance with the table below:

1 = 5
2 = 12
3 = 7
4 = 2
5 = 6

EXAMPLE:
1 = 14 (4 + 7 + 3)
4 = 8 (7 + 1)
7 = 5 (4 + 1)
3 = 1

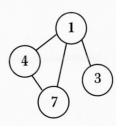

Stumper 93

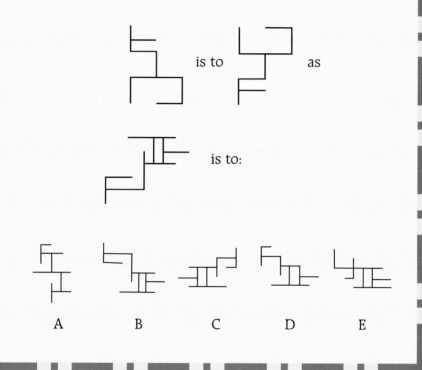

is to   as

is to:

A   B   C   D   E

Stumper 94

Arrange these words in alphabetical order.

ABOUND   ABSCOND

ABALONE   ABDOMEN

ABDICATE   ABROGATES

ABANDON

Stumper 95

Insert a word in the parentheses that means the same as the definitions outside the parentheses:

HASTEN (   ) GRASSLIKE PLANT

Stumper 96

If meat in a river (3 in 6) is T(HAM)ES,
can you find a thin rope in an instrument (4 in 9)?

Stumper 97

Arrange the letters in the squares below
to find two nine-letter words that are antonyms.

	L	A	R
R	G	E	H	G
E	N	T	I	C
E	C	I		

Stumper 98

What number should replace the question mark?

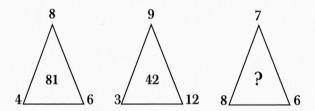

Stumper 99

The words black and white are antonyms.

What two words, one rhyming with
black and one with white, are also antonyms?

Stumper 100

Which is the missing square?

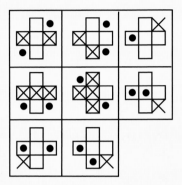

A   B   C   D

Stumper 101

Find pairs of letters to form four four-letter musical instruments—one pair is not used.

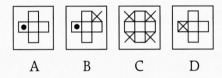

BA	HA	LU
TE	FE	OB
FI	OE	TU

Stumper 102

What number should replace
the question mark?

Simplify: $5 + 8 \div 4 + 9 \times 2 + 7 = ?$

Stumper 103

Find a six-letter word made up of
only the four following letters:

ON
IP

Stumper 104

Place two of the three-letter groups
together to form an article of clothing.

SOC - TER - COA - JER - KIT - SHI - KIN - RTY

Stumper 105

Which two words are similar in meaning?

PLUNDER, CHARM, JOSH,
WEAN, TEASE, CHANGE

Stumper 106

Which of these is the odd one out?

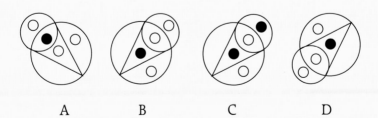

A   B   C   D

Stumper 107

Which diagram continues the sequence?

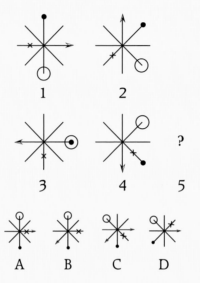

1   2

3   4   ?   5

A   B   C   D

Stumper 108

Rearrange the letters in each set
to form the name of a plant.

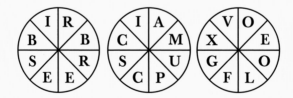

Stumper 109

Find the missing word that will fit
the rule of the example below.

CONE (NICK) KRIS
LISP (_ _ _ _) ETON

Stumper 110

A stone is dropped over the edge of a cliff.
After 5 seconds how many feet has it fallen?

A. 280 ft.
B. 320 ft.
C. 400 ft.
D. 480 ft.
E. 500 ft.

Stumper 111

Starting at a corner square, move along a spiral route and find the rule for the numbering to replace the question mark.

32	28	34	30
26	42	38	36
30	36	?	32
24	40	34	38

Stumper 112

How many revolutions are made by a 28-inch bicycle wheel over 1 mile?

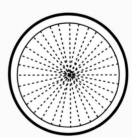

A. 620
B. 720
C. 820
D. 920
E. 1020

Stumper 113

Draw the next figure in this series.

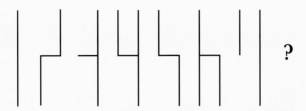 ?

Stumper 114

What is the mathematical sign for infinity?

A. ∢
B. ∞
C. Δ
D. ∷
E. ∝

Stumper 115

Fill in the blanks to find three islands:

_ H _ I _ T _ A _
_ A _ R _ T _ U _
_ A _ K _ A _ D

Stumper 116

Find a three-letter word that completes all three words on the left-hand side and prefixes all three words on the right-hand side.

HAS   DON
ROT   (_ _ _)   PIN
FAT   ANT

Stumper 117

On which target have 185 points been scored?

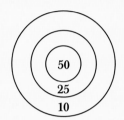

A   B   C   D

Stumper 118

Which of the following is
always part of SAUERKRAUT?

CHEESE, HOT WATER, MILK,
BUTTER, CABBAGE

Stumper 119

Place a word in the parentheses that when placed at the end of the first word makes a word and when placed in front of the second word also makes a word.

QUARTER (_ _ _ _) HAND

Stumper 120

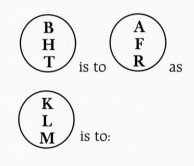

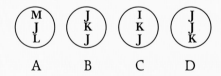

Stumper 121

Which is the odd one out?

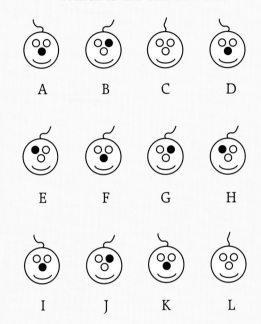

Stumper 122

Solve the anagram in parentheses
to correctly complete the quotation.
Failure is the only opportunity
to begin again, more (leniently gilt).
—Henry Ford

Stumper 123

Pair the eight words below to form four hyphenated words. Use each word once only.

GROUP, STILL, TYPING, AGE,
STOCK, SIZE, BLOOD, TWIN

Stumper 124

Mitzi has $800 to spend. She spends $2/5$ of the $800 on clothes, 0.425 of the $800 on jewelry, and writes out a check for $240 for a new watch.

What is her financial situation at the end of the day?

Stumper 125

Which word is opposite in meaning to OPTIMUM?

ANTITHESIS, UNORIGINAL,
LEAST, STARK, CHASTE

Stumper 126

What is the missing number?

5	3	8	4	9	6	8
8	6	6	1	8	4	?
3	2	7	6	8	7	3

Stumper 127

GAZEBO
ACCEDE
VERIFY

Which girl's name continues the above sequence?

A. EUNICE
B. AGATHA
C. JOANNE
D. INGRID

Stumper 128

Solve the two anagrams
to produce a well-known saying.

--- --- --- --- -- --- ---

↑THE CATTLE↑ ↑HATE BUT GOOF↑

Stumper 129

When the shape below is folded
to form a cube, just one of the
following can be produced.

Which one?

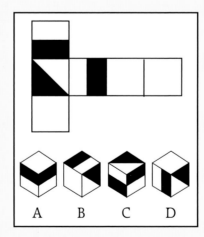

Stumper 130

If 9L of a C is 9 lives of a cat,
can you decode the following?

10P in C

Stumper 131

Solve the clues to find four six-letter words. The same
three letters are represented by XYZ in each word.

X	Y	Z	_	_	_	Clue: Fleet
_	X	Y	Z	_	_	Clue: Heat
_	_	X	Y	Z	_	Clue: Beguiles
_	_	_	X	Y	Z	Clue: Remove defensive capability

Stumper 132

What number should replace
the question mark?

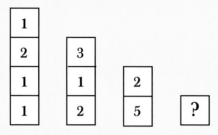

Stumper 133

The word SOLO appears only once in this grid
in a straight line. Can you find it?

It may appear horizontally, vertically
or diagonally, backwards or forwards.

S	O	L	S	L	O	S	O
S	O	S	O	S	O	O	S
O	O	S	O	S	L	O	O
O	S	O	L	S	O	O	O
S	O	S	L	S	L	L	O
L	S	L	O	O	S	O	S
O	O	O	S	S	O	O	L
O	S	L	L	O	S	L	O

Stumper 134

Spiral clockwise to find a ten-letter word. You must find the starting point and provide the missing letters. The word you are looking for starts and finishes with the same two letters.

Stumper 135

Which is the odd one out?

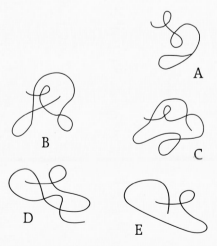

Stumper 136

We all have the ____1____ to put our ____2____ to even more use by ____3____ new avenues, experiences, and ____4____ adventures.

Select the correct words (one each) from the choices below to correctly complete the above statement.

1. PRIVILEGE, SENSE, CAPACITY, PREFERENCE, IMAGINATION
2. COMPUTERS, MONEY, ABILITY, BRAIN, VITALITY
3. EXPLORING, FINDING, ARRANGING, TOURING, CROSSING
4. DANGEROUS, MODERN, SUBTLE DISCREET, LEARNED

Stumper 137

Insert a girl's name into the bottom line and complete the three-letter words.

H	C	F	F	A	E	S	T
I	U	U	O	L	G	I	I

Stumper 138

What number should replace
the question mark?

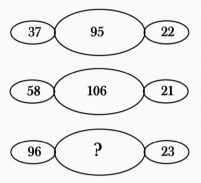

Stumper 139

DYNAMIC (ADORN) PROFUSE

Using the same rules as the example above, what
word should appear in the parentheses below?

RETORTS (_ _ _ _ _) LIBERTY

Stumper 140

What well-known phrase
is indicated below?

```
COB  LT
CO  ALT
C   BALT
COBA T
COBAL
```

Stumper 141

What is the total of the numbers
on the reverse of these dice?

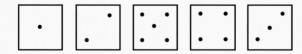

Stumper 142

Which of these is the odd one out?

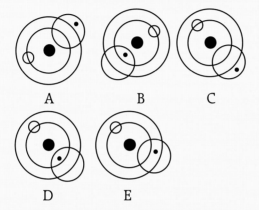

A   B   C

D   E

Stumper 143

Which of these is not an anagram of currency?

A. ZETQULEA

B. YOMASED

C. DASRUCO

D. VILBAOR

E. TATRES

F. TERECSES

Stumper 144

Find a one-word anagram in:

SORE CAT

Stumper 145

Place four of the three-letter groups
together to make two six-letter words.

SUT - TIC - NAU - TIN - HER - MET - SEA - MIT

Stumper 146

Fill in the blank spaces to spell out three dances.

_ I _ T _ R _ U _
_ U _ D _ I _ L _
_ O _ O _ A _ S _

Stumper 147

Which two words have opposite meanings?

LADYLIKE, SUCCINCT, TURBULENT,
COMMODIOUS, HOYDENISH, EMACIATED

Stumper 148

If the missing letters in the two circles below
are correctly inserted they will form synonyms.
The words do not have to be read in a clockwise direction,
but the letters are consecutive.

What are the words and missing letters?

Stumper 149

LING is to FISH as CARAVEL is to:

    A. MINSTREL
    B. CARAVAN
    C. CIRCUS
    D. VEHICLE
    E. BOAT

Stumper 150

What roman numeral should
replace the question mark?

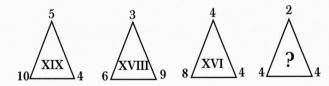

Stumper 151

What number should replace the question mark?

7   17 $8\frac{1}{2}$ $14\frac{1}{4}$ 10 $11\frac{1}{2}$?

Stumper 152

What is the meaning of MANTILLA?

A. TROUSERS
B. SHIP
C. DRESS
D. LOGANBERRIES
E. SCARF

Stumper 153

There are only five regular
solids with symmetrical faces.

Which one of these has twenty faces?

A. ICOSAHEDRON
B. DODECAHEDRON
C. CUBE
D. TETRAHEDRON
E. OCTAHEDRON

Stumper 154

How many degrees is this angle?

A. 105°
B. 110°
C. 115°
D. 120°
E. 130°

Stumper 155

What is x?

$$\frac{4 \times 2 - 6}{7 - 4 \times 2} = x$$

Stumper 156

HIPPOPHOBIA is to HORSES
as AILUROPHOBIA is to:

A. ELEPHANTS
B. LIONS
C. MICE
D. SHARKS
E. CATS

Stumper 157

Which word can be placed at the end
of these words to make new words?

STIR
KIND
SAC   (_ _ _)
BAR
HAT

Stumper 158

Complete the word.

_ _ U B R _ _ _ _

Stumper 159

Which circle's letters cannot be
rearranged into a six-letter word?

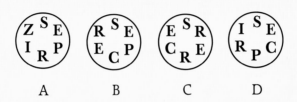

A   B   C   D

Stumper 160

NECTAR is to DRINK as AMBROSIA is to:

A. MEDICINE

B. BEES

C. GREECE

D. TONIC

E. FOOD

Stumper 161

What word should replace
the question mark?

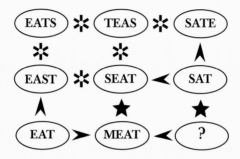

Stumper 162

What do these words have in common?

AMULET
DEMURE
MORATORIUM
MULTIGERM

Stumper 163

Consider the following square:

Now consider the following array:

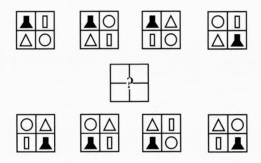

Which square should replace the question mark?

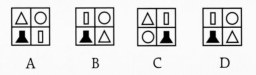

A   B   C   D

Stumper 164

"An adventurous action that runs counter to approved or conventional conduct."

What word fits closest to this definition?

A. MISDEMEANOR
B. ESCAPADE
C. EXPERIENCE
D. VENTURE
E. EXPLORATION

Stumper 165

Move from star to star to spell out a ten-letter word.

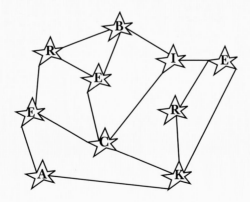

Stumper 166

Sam visited several places in Europe.

He hated Madrid.
He loved Prague.
He hated Warsaw.
He hated Antrim.
He loved Ankara.

Did he love or hate Vienna?

Stumper 167

Which number is the odd one out?

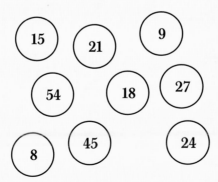

Stumper 168

Find the starting point and visit each square once to reach the treasure marked T.

1N 2W
= 1 North
2 West

N
W——+——E
S

1S 1E	1S 1E	2S
1S	**T**	1N 2W
1E 2N	2N 1E	2W 1N

Stumper 169

Which is the odd one out?

ACETATE
NYLON
POLYESTER
VICUNA
RAYON

Stumper 170

Solve each anagram to find two phrases
that are spelled differently but sound alike.
For example: a name, an aim.

IDLE LURES   ROSY DOLL

Stumper 171

Insert two words that are anagrams of each other
to complete the sentence. For example: She
removed the <u>stain</u> from her new <u>satin</u> blouse.

Cheated out of what was rightfully mine,
it would be a long, hard battle before I
could _____ my inheritance. My solicitor
warned me I could only hope for a _____,
but I was determined to fight to the bitter end.

Stumper 172

What number is three places away from itself plus 4,
two places away from itself minus 3, three places
from itself doubled, two places away from itself
minus 1, three places away from itself plus 3,
and two places away from itself minus 5?

19	14	3	8	11
9	2	20	6	5
15	22	16	2	30
24	7	18	4	10
18	1	12	13	17

Stumper 173

Which shape continues the sequence below?

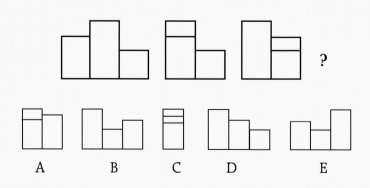

A   B   C   D   E

Stumper 174

Underline the two words in parentheses that the word outside the parentheses always has.

RIVER (ESTUARY, WATER,
BOATS, MOVEMENT, WATERFALL)

Stumper 175

What letter should replace the question mark?

Stumper 176

Which is the missing section?

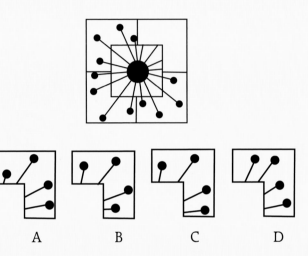

A   B   C   D

Stumper 177

The cost of hiring a private rail carriage is shared equally by all the passengers. The carriage has seats for forty passengers and the total bill amounts to $70.37.

How many passenger seats are not occupied?

Stumper 178

What word is indicated from the clues below?

The bottom of the heap,
The end of the line,
The first of all,
The center of artichoke,
The beginning of the end.

Stumper 179

Divide 800 by $\frac{1}{4}$ and add 5.

What is the answer?

Stumper 180

Rearrange the tiles so that every two horizontally adjacent letters form a word, and two related words can be read around the outer edge.

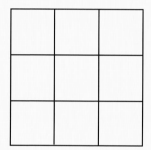

Stumper 181

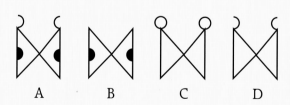

A   B   C   D

Stumper 182

Place the letters in the grid
to make a color and a lizard.

A A G H I K K N U I

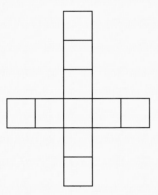

Stumper 183

What number comes next in the series?

0.5	A. 0.857
0.666	B. 0.861
0.75	C. 0.865
0.8	D. 0.869
0.833	E. 0.873

Stumper 184

What is the name given to a group of turtles?

A. TRAIL
B. SHELL
C. KNOT
D. WADDLE
E. BALE
F. NEST

Stumper 185

Place three of the two-letter groups together to form a bird.

AN - IN - PI - DU - GE - NL

Stumper 186

Simplify:

Stumper 187

Which is the odd one out?

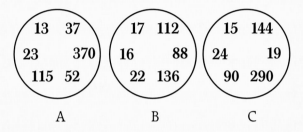

A   B   C

Stumper 188

There is an odd letter in each hexagon.

Can you find them?

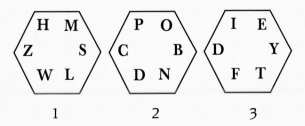

1   2   3

Stumper 189

Which of these is not a bird?

    A. PUFFIN
    B. SISKIN
    C. CALABASH
    D. MALLARD
    E. MERLIN
    F. GOSHAWK

Stumper 190

Find a twelve-letter bird made
up of two six-letter words.

Six letters inside
Six letters outside

Stumper 191

What symbol should continue the series?

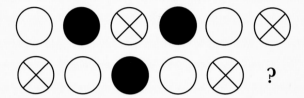

?

Stumper 192

By moving through the doorways,
spell out an eight-letter word.

Stumper 193

Which word means the fear of travel?

    A. HODOPHOBIA
    B. NELOPHOBIA
    C. IDEOPHOBIA
    D. ANDROPHOBIA
    E. HYDROPHOBIA

Stumper 194

Find three animals hidden
in the following sentence:

"In the current times everyone will be
a saver at least once with a pension."

Stumper 195

How many degrees are there in this angle?

A. 100°
B. 105°
C. 108°
D. 110°
E. 120°

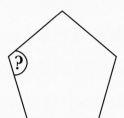

Stumper 196

What number should replace
the question mark below?

Stumper 197

Fill in the missing letters to make a
nine-letter word, starting from a corner square
and continuing in a spiral to the center.

	E	I
I	D	N
A	R	

Stumper 198

How many different teams of eleven players
can be selected from fifteen members?

Stumper 199

Fill in the missing letter to fit
the rule of this pattern.

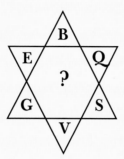

Stumper 200

Change this fraction to a decimal.

$$\frac{3}{8} = \; ?$$

Stumper 201

Complete the grid with the letters MAGIC so that no row, column, or diagonal line contains the same letter more than once.

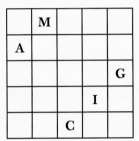

Stumper 202

I have correctly and accurately made a clear impact with the crown of a small fastener.

What have I done?

Stumper 203

If a car had increased its average speed
for a 210-mile journey by 5 mph the journey
would have been completed in 1 hour less.

What was the original speed of
the car for the journey?

Stumper 204

Which is the odd one out?

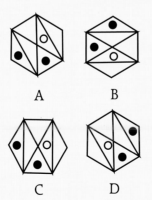

A   B

C   D

Stumper 205

What number should replace
the question mark?

9	4	6	11
3	6	7	4
5	?	4	1
11	6	3	8

Stumper 206

Add three consecutive letters of the alphabet to
the group of letters below, without splitting the
consecutive letters, to form another word.

DY

Stumper 207

Which word is opposite in meaning to CORPULENT?

OVERWROUGHT, COMMUNAL,
HEALTHY, POOR, GAUNT

Stumper 208

Which one of the following is not an
anagram of LITTLE GIANT ENCYCLOPEDIA?

POLITICALLY DECENT EATING
ENTICED PATIENT LOGICALLY
IDENTICALLY ELECTING POET
ALLOCATED NICE TINY PIGLET
TANGENTIALLY CITED POLICE
DETECTING ALIAN OPTICALLY

Stumper 209

Which month comes next?

JANUARY, MARCH, JUNE,
OCTOBER, MARCH, ?

Stumper 210

What letter should replace the question mark?

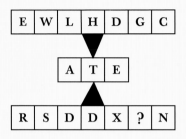

E	W	L	H	D	G	C

A	T	E

R	S	D	D	X	?	N

Stumper 211

Which circles should replace
the ones with the question mark?

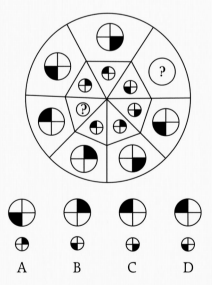

Stumper 212

What number should replace
the question mark in the circle?

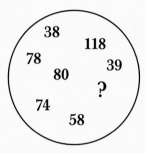

Stumper 213

Seven synonyms of the keyword are shown. Take
one letter from each of the seven synonyms in turn
to spell out an eighth synonym of the keyword.

Keyword: TALENT

Synonyms: GIFT, ABILITY, KNACK,
GENIUS, FLAIR, APTITUDE, CAPACITY

Stumper 214

Following the rule of the sequence of numbers, what number should come next?

1, 4, 7, 11, 15, 13, 17, ?

Stumper 215

REAR (LORRAINE) LION

What girl's name should go in the parentheses below according to the same rules as in the example above?

REIN (   ) AGOG

Stumper 216

Which is the odd one out?

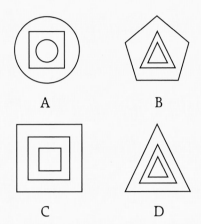

A   B

C   D

Stumper 217

Four balls are placed in a row. The red ball is next
to the green ball but not next to the blue ball.
The yellow ball is not next to the blue ball.
What ball is next to the yellow ball?

A. The red ball
B. The green ball
C. The red and the green ball
D. There is insufficient information to determine

Stumper 218

One letter in each word of a
well-known saying has been changed.

What is the saying?

OLD ORE NUT

Stumper 219

"An indirect, ingenious, and often
cunning means to gain an end."

What word most closely fits the above definition?

PLAN, STRATAGEM, EXPEDIENCY,
DIVERSION, FRAUD

Stumper 220

Taking the respective numerical position of letters in the alphabet, decode the series of numbers in the box.

$$135144512191915814$$

For example: LITTLE GIANT = 12920201257911420

```
 L   I   T   T   L   E    G   I   A   N   T
12   9  20  20  12   5    7   9   1  14  20
```

Stumper 221

What number comes next in the series?

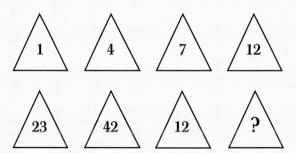

Stumper 222

What number should replace
the question mark?

Stumper 223

Find the missing word that will
fit the rule of the example below.

ROPE (PART) ANTE
SHAM (_ _ _ _) PIER

Stumper 224

If 3 × 6 = 24,
then 4 × 3 = ?

Stumper 225

What is the missing number?

24	1	4	3
18	1	4	1
30	1	4	?

Stumper 226

Starting at an outside square and moving in any direction, spell out a ten-letter name of a girl.

EG	NA	MO
AR	LD	RA
DE	BO	HI

Stumper 227

A word can be placed in the parentheses that has the same meaning as the words outside.

What is it? Each dash represents a letter.

STEAL (_ _ _ _ _) COOK IN WATER

Stumper 228

The Beaufort wind scale is numbered from 0 to 17.

Which number denotes a storm?

A. 8
B. 9
C. 10
D. 11
E. 12

Stumper 229

Trace out a ten-letter word in any direction, using each letter once only.

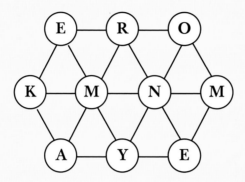

Stumper 230

Place four of the three-letter groups together to make two six-letter words.

TTI - VIS - CAN - DER - ODI - MUR - OUS - SEC

Stumper 231

What is the mathematical
sign for arc of a circle?

A. →
B. ●
C. ∪
D. ⌒
E. ▭

Stumper 232

What number should replace
the question mark?

1   12   3¼   10½   5½   9   7¾   ?

Stumper 233

Complete the word.

_ _ _ G H C _ _ _

Stumper 234

Simplify $\dfrac{675}{1000}$ as a fraction.

Stumper 235

Fill in the blanks to find four girls' names.

A		N		E
E				I
E		I		A

Stumper 236

Find the complete word that contains these middle letters. The word is hyphenated.

Z Z Y W

Stumper 237

Fill in the spaces to spell out three occupations.

_ I _ N _ L _ A _
_ O _ D _ L _ E _
_ A _ N _ Q _ I _

Stumper 238

Complete the sequence.

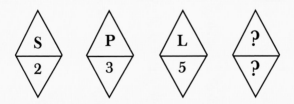

Stumper 239

Which word will fit in front of
these words to make new words?

(_ _ _)
HEAD
PRICK
STRIPE
BALL
CUSHION

Stumper 240

With a standard six-sided die, how many
throws are required on average before each
of the six numbers has landed faceup?

A. 10
B. 15
C. 20
D. 25

Stumper 241

Which four of the five pieces below
can be used to construct a perfect circle?

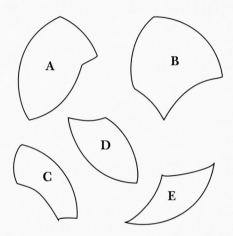

Stumper 242

Which two of the following
words are closest in meaning?

EXOTERIC, RECONDITE, PLAIN,
DARK, REASONABLE, ROSEATE

Stumper 243

Arrange the letters in the squares to find two nine-letter words that are antonyms.

		U	R	P
V	D	R	T	O
S	R	E	S	P
Y	A	A		

Stumper 244

In which of the sentences below does the name of an animal not appear?

A. I was suddenly confronted by a group of evil-doers and hardened criminals.
B. Their leader was well-dressed and swarthy, wearing thick-rimmed, tinted spectacles.
C. "Who is this?" said a small, squat individual. "I don't trust him; he could be armed."
D. The leader roared with laughter and gesticulated with his bejewelled arm. "Believe me, he is quite harmless," he said, "but escort him from the premises immediately."
E. I walked out into the cold night air with a huge sigh of relief. This time I had avoided the trap easily, but I knew I might not be so lucky next time.

Stumper 245

What number should replace
the question mark?

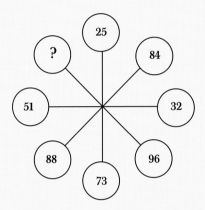

Stumper 246

What letter is immediately to the left of
the letter two to the right of the letter four to the
left of the letter two to the right of the letter C?

Stumper 247

Which is the odd one out?

REAMER, GIMLET, CLEAVER,
WIMBLE, AUGER

Stumper 248

Which numbers should replace
the question marks?

78	64	62	48	46	32
79	67	63	51	47	35
76	?	?	50	44	34
74	?	?	52	42	36
75	71	59	55	43	39
72	70	56	54	40	38

66	61		66	61		66	60		64	61
69	58		68	56		68	58		69	56

A   B   C   D

Stumper 249

Place two of the three-letter
groups together to form a food.

POT - MEL - CAR - SLI - OAT - WHE - MUE - ATE

Stumper 250

What do the following words have in common?

APPROPRIATE
BOW
DESERT
DOVE
ENTRANCE
GILL
LEAD
SLAVER

Stumper 251

You have a range of weights available from
1 to 10. They are all single weights. Which one
should you use to balance the 10 ft. scale,
and where should you place it?

Stumper 252

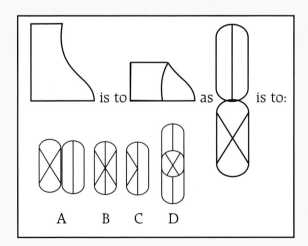

Stumper 253

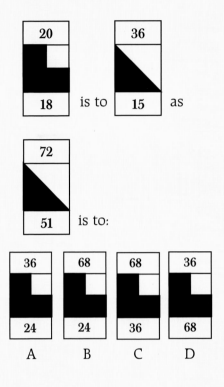

is to ... as

is to:

36 / 24 — A
68 / 24 — B
68 / 36 — C
36 / 68 — D

Stumper 254

Think of a four-letter word that reverses its meaning when the letter "T" is placed in front of it.

Stumper 255

Place a word in the parentheses that when placed at the end of the first word makes a word and when placed in front of the second word also makes a word.

OPERA (_ _) US

Stumper 256

The following is extracted from what hyphenated word?

_ _ _ _ S – EX _ _ _ _ _ _ _ _ _

Clue: Third degree

Stumper 257

SHORT LANCE is an anagram of which American city?

Stumper 258

In a game of six players that lasts for 50 minutes,
two reserves substitute for each player so that
all players, including reserves, are on the
field for the same length of time.

How long is each player on the field?

Stumper 259

What comes next in the below sequence?

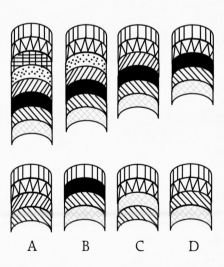

A   B   C   D

Stumper 260

OVERUSED : CLICHÉD
OVERATTENTIVE :

CHINTZY, SCHOLASTIC,
IRRITABLE, IMPERIOUS, OFFICIOUS

Stumper 261

What is the meaning of TULLE?

A. VEGETABLE
B. SILK FABRIC
C. A MYSTIC
D. TENSILE
E. WEAPON

Stumper 262

Fill in the blanks to find three minerals.

_ L _ M _ N _ M
_ A _ N _ S _ U _
_ A _ G _ N _ S _

Stumper 263

Find a one-word anagram
from the two words below.

DEEP DRESS

Stumper 264

Which word continues this sequence?

SON, EAT, WORTH, ?

A. REEL
B. LUNG
C. DEATH
D. PINE

Stumper 265

Which arrangement of pipes
would carry most water?

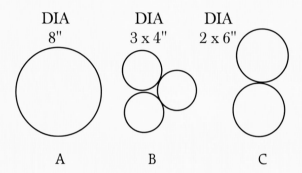

DIA
8"

DIA
3 x 4"

DIA
2 x 6"

A   B   C

Stumper 266

Which are the odd ones out?

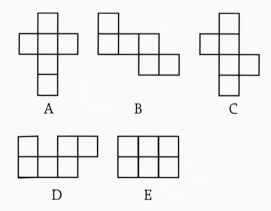

A   B   C

D   E

Stumper 267

Which of the following metals is
always associated with GALVANIZING?

A. COPPER
B. BRONZE
C. ZINC
D. LEAD
E. SILVER

Stumper 268

By moving through the doorways
spell out an eight-letter word.

Stumper 269

Make one word using all ten letters.

TRIBE COSTS

Clue: Pertaining to midwifery

Stumper 270

If the missing letters in the circle are correctly inserted they will form an eight-letter word. The word will not have to be read in a clockwise direction, but the letters are consecutive.

What is the word and missing letters?

Stumper 271

What number will replace
the question mark?

28   47   85   ?   218   313   427

Stumper 272

A well-known phrase has had all its vowels
removed and has been split into groups
of three letters. What is the phrase?
All remaining letters are in the correct order.

HRT DYG NTM RRW

Stumper 273

What number should replace the question mark?

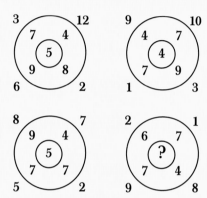

Stumper 274

Find a three-letter word that completes
all three words on the left-hand side and
prefixes all three words on the right-hand side.

PAR   EYE
HAT   (_ _ _)   HOT
MAR   DEN

Stumper 275

Fill in the missing letters to
name a group of ducks.

_ A _ D _ I _ G

Stumper 276

What is the opposite of PIETY?

A. SOLACE
B. HOLINESS
C. GOODNESS
D. IRREVERENCE
E. PASSION

Stumper 277

Find a twelve-letter fruit made
up of two six-letter words.

One word inside
One word outside

Stumper 278

Place two of the three-letter groups
together to make a six-letter vehicle.

OPY - SED - WAG - ONE - JAL - ANN

Stumper 279

The vowels have been omitted from this quotation. See if you can put them back in.

THFMLYTHTPRYSTGTHRSTYSTGTHR

Stumper 280

What number should replace
the question mark?

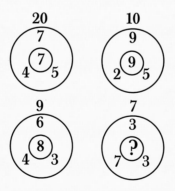

Stumper 281

What comes next?

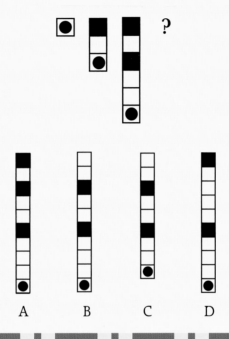

A   B   C   D

Stumper 282

What number is missing from the left-hand circle?

Stumper 283

Add one letter, not necessarily the same letter, to each word to find two words that are opposite in meaning.

SEND HARD

Stumper 284

Pair the eight words below to form four longer words.

IRON, LOAD, FIRE, WORK, MAIN, GRID, WOOD, LAND

Stumper 285

Find the number to replace the question mark.

369542 is to 246359 as
172896 is to 268179 as
417638 is to ?

Stumper 286

What do these words have in common?

LIBERATION
CHINCHILLA
INITIALLY
SPEARMINT
FRAGRANCE
PERFUME
CLAUSTROPHOBIA

Stumper 287

What letter should replace
the question mark?

18	4	22
S	E	?
7	21	3

Stumper 288

Insert the letters of the phrase AN AGENT'S GAMMA into the following blanks only once each to complete a palindromic sentence, that is, one that reads the same backwards and forwards. For example, MADAM, I'M ADAM.

_ _ T _ _ _ _ ' _ _ _ _ E _ _ _

Clue: Doorkeeper's ID

Stumper 289

DAWN is to DAY as WINTER is to:

AUTUMN, SEASON, NIGHT, SPRING, SUMMER

Stumper 290

What phrase is indicated here?

O
V
E
R

Stumper 291

What number should replace
the question mark?

2	3	4	2
6	1	4	4
4	2	2	5
5	3	7	?

Stumper 292

Solve the clues to find four six-letter words. The same three letters are represented by XYZ in each word.

XYZ _ _ _	Clue: Falls
_ XYZ _ _	Clue: Hangs fabric
_ _ XYZ _	Clue: Graze
_ _ _ XYZ	Clue: Snare

Stumper 293

Which two words that sound alike
but are spelled differently mean:

SOLITARY, ADVANCE?

Stumper 294

What are the missing letters:

Stumper 295

Fill in the missing word in the crossword below:

Stumper 296

Which is the odd one out?

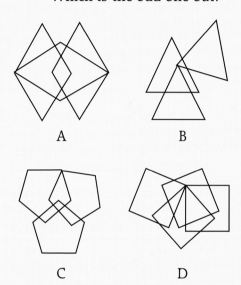

A   B

C   D

Stumper 297

Which is the odd word out?

COMPRESS
DIMINISH
EBB
VANISH
DEPLETE

Stumper 298

Fill in the consonants to complete our
words that have the same meaning.

_ E _ E _ O U _
_ _ A _ I _ A _ L _
_ E _ E _ O _ E _ _
_ I _ _

Clue: Openhanded

Stumper 299

Move from letter to letter horizontally
and vertically, but not diagonally, to spell
out a twelve-letter word. You have to find the
starting point and provide the missing letters.

	M	M	E
R	I		N
I	S	O	

Stumper 300

Place the letters in the grid to make a
warm-blooded and a cold-blooded animal.

A A E K L L M S T

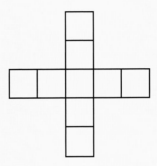

Stumper 301

Which four-letter word placed inside
the parentheses will complete these words?

(_ _ _ _) RAL   E (_ _ _ _) NT

Stumper 302

Place two of the four-letter
groups together to make a word.

TURN - EFUL - TACE - WACK - SPIT - INGS

Stumper 303

Which word will carry on the sequence?

HALF-MAST, TAVERNER, RIPARIAN,
NOBILITY, YULETIDE, ?

A. DOUBLOON
B. EXCITING
C. MACARONI
D. OVERTONE
E. SKY PILOT
F. TICKLISH

Stumper 304

Find a six-letter word made up of
only the following four letters.

AJ

MP

Stumper 305

Change this fraction to a decimal.

$$\frac{7}{8} =$$

Stumper 306

LEG is to FIBULA as ARM is to:

A. COCCYX
B. THORAX
C. CLAVICLE
D. ULNA
E. SCAPULA

Stumper 307

Rearrange the two five-letter words to form
a ten-letter word meaning "kind to strangers."

HABIT POLES

Stumper 308

Which of the following is
associated with HASLET?

A. PATE
B. BREAD
C. ENTRAILS
D. KIPPERS
E. GINGER

Stumper 309

Which word can be placed on the
end of these words to make new words?

PILL
POT
GARB   (_ _ _)
FOOT
DAM

Stumper 310

What is the symbol for CHROMIUM?

A. C
B. Ch
C. Cr
D. Cm
E. Chm

Stumper 311

Fill in the missing letters
to name a group of cats.

_ L _ T _ E _

Stumper 312

Fill in the missing letters to
spell out different foods.

_ A _ B _ R _ E _
_ I _ C _ M _ A _
_ P _ G _ E _ T _

Stumper 313

What is the opposite of ÉCLAT?

A. ENHANCE
B. ILLUME
C. CRAMPED
D. DEMENTIA
E. DISAPPROVAL

Stumper 314

Make up four pairs of words to find the odd one.

TOKEN
ICE
GREEN
SQUARE
SALTS
PEPPERS
FLOE
MAGIC
BATH

Stumper 315

What is associated with GNOCCHI?

A. SARDINES

B. STRAWBERRIES

C. MELONS

D. TAPIOCA

E. DUMPLINGS

Stumper 316

To what does the adjective DIACONAL refer?

A. DIAMOND SHAPED
B. TEACHER
C. CONVERSATION
D. DEACON
E. WEALTH

Stumper 317

DELTIOLOGY is the study of

A. RIVER MOUTHS
B. PICTURE POSTCARDS
C. BRIDGES
D. PRISONS
E. FINGERS

Stumper 318

One man can mow a lawn in 6 hours,
and another man can mow the same lawn
in 3 hours. If they both worked together at
their respective rates, how long would they take?

Stumper 319

PISSIFORM is to PEA SHAPED
as CLAVIFORM is to:

A. CROSS SHAPED
B. WEB SHAPED
C. CLUB SHAPED
D. SQUARE SHAPED
E. SWORD SHAPED

Stumper 320

What number should replace
the question mark?

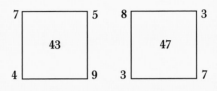

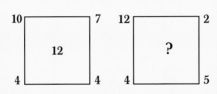

7 ⎾ ⎤ 5   8 ⎾ ⎤ 3
   43   47
4 ⎿ ⎦ 9   3 ⎿ ⎦ 7

10 ⎾ ⎤ 7   12 ⎾ ⎤ 2
   12   ?
4 ⎿ ⎦ 4   4 ⎿ ⎦ 5

Answers

TEST 1
TRIVIAL

TEST 2
8. The top number is the product of the bottom numbers divided by 15.

TEST 3
TORRENTIAL

TEST 4
C. It is the only one that doesn't have an identical match.

TEST 5
The number of votes the winning candidate received was (963 + 53 + 79 + 105) ÷ 4 = 300. The second received 300 - 53 = 247, the third received 300 - 79 = 221, and the fourth received 300 - 105 = 195.

TEST 6
REDEVELOP, PENTAGRAM

TEST 7
FINE AND DANDY

TEST 8
ALOUD, ALLOWED

TEST 9
FANCIFUL, SENSIBLE

TEST 10
E. ARIES : RAM

TEST 11
WEASEL

TEST 12
E. The lines of the third pentagon are determined by the lines of the first two. All lines are carried forward, but when two lines coincide in the same position in the first two figures they appear as a curved line in the final figure.

TEST 13
COCKATRICE, BASILISK

TEST 14
44. The rule is multiplication and division before addition and subtraction.

TEST 15
AIM DRAG = DIAGRAM. The buildings are STADIUM, LIBRARY, HOSPITAL, and PAVILION.

TEST 16
HORN

TEST 17
E. LILY

TEST 18
64. The bottom number is the top right number times the square root of the top left number.

TEST 19
LESSEE, LANDLORD

TEST 20
B

TEST 21
523377. All the others, when split into two three-digit numbers, add up to 1000. (For example, 586 + 414 = 1000.)

TEST 22
BEAGLE

TEST 23
INSPECTS, EXAMINES

TEST 24
TIRELESSLY

TEST 25
B. Lines in the outer circle move 45° clockwise at each stage. Lines in the middle circle move 45° counterclockwise at each stage. The line in the inner circle moves 45° clockwise at each stage.

TEST 26
A. If a segment is folded on top of the opposite segment, numbers on top of each other total 10. (For example, the top segment folds onto the bottom segment so that the 8 covers the 2, the 5 covers the 5, and the 7 covers the 3.)

TEST 27
151. The difference between two consecutive squares is the sum of the two numbers being squared. So this is simply 76 + 75.

TEST 28
MARTIAL, MARSHAL

TEST 29
A. TAPERING TO A POINT

TEST 30
C. Each symbol alternates between black and white or black and gray. The circles on the right move from corner to corner, one clockwise, one counterclockwise.

TEST 31
Mixed fortunes

TEST 32
13. Starting at 1 and moving two segments clockwise yields the series 1, 2, 3, 5, 8, ?, 21. Each term of the series is the sum of the previous two terms.

TEST 33
VIOLIN: This is a string instrument, the rest are wind instruments.

TEST 34
SPLENETIC, HAPPY

TEST 35
MILWAUKEE

TEST 36
B. ILLUMINATION : LIGHT

TEST 37
EGLANTINE, BRIER

TEST 38
TIE

TEST 39
E. The second number is the first digit of the first number times the second digit of the first number plus the third digit of the first number. 26 = 8 × 3 + 2.

TEST 40
B. In each row and column, the third circle is the first and second circle superimposed, with overlapping parts removed.

TEST 41
17271. Each term in the series is the first two digits of the previous term times the last three digits of the previous term. So 17271 = 19 × 909.

TEST 42
INVENTOR, DESIGNER

TEST 43
BROWN, ORANGE, BLUE

TEST 44
ACT

TEST 45
EQUESTRIAN

TEST 46
NAÏVE, SLY

TEST 47
E. It contains one large circle, three medium circles, two small white circles, and two small black circles.

TEST 48
RATIONAL

TEST 49
SAGACIOUS, FOOLISH

TEST 50
ALTER, ALTAR

TEST 51
B. In all the others, the top half is a mirror image of the bottom half.

TEST 52
C. NIZNAI = ZINNIA. The gems are ZIRCON, DIAMOND, SAPPHIRE, and JACINTH.

TEST 53
7. The center number is the product of the top two numbers divided by the bottom number.

TEST 54
OXYGEN

TEST 55
WEAPON

TEST 56
SWIMMING: The others require a ball.

TEST 57
MAGNETIC, ALLURING

TEST 58
1. Starting at the first 1 and moving one segment clockwise yields the series 1, ?, 2, 4, 7, 11, 16, 22. The difference between terms of the series increases by 1; that is, the differences are 0, 1, 2, 3, 4, 5, and 6.

TEST 59
D. SAPPHIRE : BLUE

TEST 60
1C

TEST 61
D. The second and third numbers are 909 greater than the numbers to their left.

TEST 62
VOLUME: It has an alternating consonant and vowel arrangement.

TEST 63
COUNCIL, CONCLAVE

TEST 64
SON OF A GUN

TEST 65
F. Moving across, the letters jump two, then three places in the alphabet. Moving down, they jump three, then four places.

TEST 66
TANGO, WALTZ, RUMBA

TEST 67
ESCORTED, ATTENDED

TEST 68
D. ALPHA : OMEGA

TEST 69
B. All the others are the same figure rotated.

TEST 70
C. ADORNTO = TORNADO. The clouds are CIRRUS, ALTOSTRATUS, CUMULUS, and NIMBUS.

TEST 71
PITTANCE (small amount). All the others have to do with crime.

TEST 72
FRATERNITY

TEST 73
WINE

TEST 74
D. The figures move two corners clockwise at each stage and are being repeated, but black instead of white.

TEST 75
DEEP BLUE

TEST 76
36. Starting at 4 and moving three segments counterclockwise yields the sequence 4, 9, 16, 25, ?, 49, 64. These are perfect squares: 2^2, 3^2, 4^2, 5^2, 6^2, 7^2, 8^2.

TEST 77
D. 2500 sq. yd. Each side is 50 yards.

TEST 78
OFF

TEST 79
COMMODIOUS, CRAMPED

TEST 80
C. The second circle is the first one rotated 180°.

TEST 81
RELEVANT, APPOSITE

TEST 82
STUBBORN, FLEXIBLE

TEST 83
131. The center number is the sum of the squares of the outer numbers. $131 = 1^2 + 7^2 + 9^2$.

TEST 84
C. The total for C is 62. The total for both A and D is 60, and the total for both B and E is 147. C is the only one that doesn't have an identical match.

TEST 85
INCOMPETENT, ADEQUATE

TEST 86
D. The black dot moves two corners counter-clockwise at each stage. The triangle moves two sides clockwise at each stage and alternates being inside and outside the pentagon. The rectangle moves one side counterclockwise at each stage and alternates being inside and outside the pentagon.

TEST 87
POSTPONE, ADVANCE

TEST 88
D

TEST 89
E. WOOL : ANGORA

TEST 90
MADISON

TEST 91
CUT FIGURE

TEST 92
REREDOS (a decorated wall in a church). All the others have to do with cooking.

TEST 93
MEMORABLE DATE

TEST 94
41. The center number is the difference between the products of the two diagonals. $41 = (13 \times 7) - (10 \times 5)$.

TEST 95
ORIGINATOR

TEST 96
BAG

TEST 97
-21. The rule is parentheses first, then multiplication and division before addition and subtraction.

TEST 98
DRAGON

TEST 99
BEAT, BEET

TEST 100
E. Each circle is made by superimposing the two circles below it and removing overlapping parts.

TEST 101
PAN

TEST 102
COSMIC (COMIC)

TEST 103
D. In each row and column, the third square is the first and second square superimposed, with overlapping parts removed.

TEST 104
ENTIRELY, SLIGHTLY

TEST 105
55. Each number is the number above it times 3 plus either 2, 3, or 4, depending on which column it is. $55 = 17 \times 3 + 4$. $169 = 55 \times 3 + 4$.

TEST 106
BERNADETTE

TEST 107
SATURATE, DOUSE

TEST 108
STOWAWAY

TEST 109
A. The rectangle and square swap places and the center item in each stays on the side that it was on.

TEST 110
DIRECT

TEST 111
ONLOOKER

TEST 112
CHASTE, CHASED

TEST 113
PERSIMMON (fruit). All the others have to do with poetry.

TEST 114
21. Starting at 6 and moving three segments clockwise yields the sequence 6, 7, 9, 12, 16, ?, 27. The difference between terms in the sequence increases by 1 each time.

TEST 115
126. $(9! \div (5! \times 4!))$. $n! = 1 \times 2 \times 3 \times 4 \times ... \times n$.

TEST 116
DEXTERITY, CLUMSINESS

TEST 117
Change of heart

TEST 118
C. LOWLIP = PILLOW. The trees are POPLAR, WILLOW, LARCH, and DEODAR.

TEST 119
E. The left halves of the second and third numbers are formed by adding the first and third digits of the previous number. The right halves are formed by adding the second and fourth digits of the previous number. $12 = 3 + 9$, $15 = 7 + 8$, $2 = 1 + 1$, $7 = 2 + 5$.

TEST 120
E

TEST 121
E. The figures change ABCDEFG to FCEAGBD.

TEST 122
SIDE, SIGHED

TEST 123
LINEN

TEST 124
D. In each row and column, the third square is the overlapping parts of the superimposed first and second squares.

TEST 125
LICENSE TO MARKET

TEST 126
WORK

TEST 127
DIRT: All of the words have their letters in alphabetical order.

TEST 128
INTERMEDIATE

TEST 129
74. The center number is the sum of the reversals of the outer numbers. $74 = 37 + 12 + 25$.

TEST 130
D

TEST 131
CLEMENT

TEST 132
15. The center number is the sum of the top left number, the top right number, and the lower right number, minus the lower left number. $15 = 17 + 4 + 9 - 15$.

TEST 133
UP TO DATE

TEST 134
ASTRINGENT, SEPARATING

TEST 135
CHAFF

TEST 136
HEXAGON: It is a planar figure; the rest are solid figures.

TEST 137
INTIMATE, INDICATE

TEST 138
NELSON

TEST 139
COL, DEPRESSION

TEST 140
2B

TEST 141
SOUVENIR, KEEPSAKE

TEST 142
3096. The center number in a row is the product of the digits on the left followed by the product of the digits on the right. $30 = 5 \times 2 \times 3$; $96 = 8 \times 2 \times 6$.

TEST 143
A. SCI SOAP = PICASSO. The composers are ROSSINI, COPLAND, WAGNER, and MAHLER.

TEST 144
C. It contains circles of three different sizes with a black dot in all of them.

TEST 145
The top number is the product of the two previous numbers. The bottom number is the sum of the two previous numbers. $30 = 6 \times 5$; $11 = 6 + 5$.

TEST 146
B. ABBREVIATIONS, UNDERSTOOD

TEST 147
ADVENTURER

TEST 148
25622. All the others are three-digit numbers followed by their square roots. For example, 67626 is 676 followed by 26, which is the square root of 676.

TEST 149
EPHEMERAL, BRIEF

TEST 150
COB: This is a male animal; the rest are female.

TEST 151
CORD, CHORD

TEST 152
CHAPTER

TEST 153
4. The center number is the difference between the sum of the left three numbers and the sum of the right three numbers. $4 = (6 + 11 + 2) - (5 + 9 + 1)$.

TEST 154
SOUP

TEST 155
DIMINUTIVE, GARGANTUAN

TEST 156
PAVANE

TEST 157
$\frac{5}{3}$ or $1\frac{2}{3}$.

TEST 158
SEAWEED

TEST 159
SAUERKRAUT (cabbage). All the others are sausages.

TEST 160
C. In each row and column, the third circle is the first and second circle superimposed, with overlapping parts removed.

TEST 161
C. All the others are the same figure rotated.

TEST 162
D. SQUARE : OCTAGON. An octagon has double the number of sides of a square and a hexagon has double the number of sides of a triangle.

TEST 163
$3500 = 50 \times 70$. $50 = 5 + 9 + 3 + 17 + 1 + 15$; $70 = 4 + 10 + 2 + 14 + 32 + 8$.

TEST 164
BOUND: The vowels A, E, I, O, and U are being repeated in order.

TEST 165
B. The large arc moves 90° counterclockwise at each stage. The middle arc moves 90° clockwise at each stage. The inner arc moves 90° clockwise at each stage.

TEST 166
15. In each row and column, the third number is the product of the first two numbers divided by four.

TEST 167
DEMOCRATIC

TEST 168
CONFUSED

TEST 169
ROME WAS NOT BUILT IN A DAY.

TEST 170
REST

TEST 171
THRILL

TEST 172
$131\frac{5}{8}$. Each term is $-1\frac{1}{2}$ times the previous term.

TEST 173
MASTER

TEST 174
26. Starting at 10 and moving three segments clockwise yields the series 10, 11, 14, 19, ?, 35, 46. The difference between terms in the series is the sequence of odd numbers, 1, 3, 5, 7, 9, 11.

TEST 175
DRAGOMAN, INTERPRETER

TEST 176
BEECH, BEACH

TEST 177
TANKER: It is engine driven; the rest use sails.

TEST 178
CHAT

TEST 179
D. TUBERT = BUTTER. The flowers are DAFFODIL, TULIP, GLADIOLI and PANSY.

TEST 180
A. Each part moves a fixed number of degrees clockwise, either 0, 90, or 180.

TEST 181
C. It contains five small white circles and four black circles, while the rest contain four small white circles and five black circles.

TEST 182
VOLATILE, CONSTANT

TEST 183
B. 96. The numbers are successive perfect squares (1, 4, 9, 16, 25, 36, 49, 64) split into groups of two numbers.

TEST 184
SUGGESTION

TEST 185
MINIMAL

TEST 186
B. At each stage the black dot moves 45° counterclockwise, the small white circle moves clockwise 90°, the medium size circle moves clockwise 90°, and the large circle moves clockwise 45°.

TEST 187
C. OROLOGY : MOUNTAINS. Orology is a branch of geology dealing with mountains, and seismology is a branch of science dealing with earthquakes.

TEST 188
OVERWHELM

TEST 189
N. Starting with A, the sequence alternates between skipping two letters and one letter.

TEST 190
BUILD, BILLED

TEST 191
FILE

TEST 192
9. The center number is the product of the upper left, upper right, and lower right numbers, divided by the lower left number. $9 = 9 \times 3 \times 4 \div 12$.

TEST 193
FAVEOLATE (honeycombed). All the others have to do with wind.

TEST 194
LANCINATE, MEND

TEST 195
D. GENORA = ORANGE. The vegetables are POTATO, CABBAGE, SPROUTS, and CARROT.

TEST 196
DULCIMER

TEST 197
There is a 50% chance that two coins will land heads up. It is a certainty that at least two coins will end up with the same side up. Thus it is just as likely that those two coins will be heads as it is that they will be tails.

TEST 198
FEMALE DONKEY

TEST 199
IRON

TEST 200
E. Each circle is made by superimposing the two circles below it and removing overlapping parts.

TEST 201
11. The center number is the difference between the upper right number and the lower left number divided by the difference between the upper left number and the lower right number. $11 = (89 - 56) \div (21 - 18)$.

TEST 202
GOPHER

TEST 203
D. It is the only one that doesn't have an identical match. A is the same figure as B. C is the same figure as E

TEST 204
INTRINSIC, NATIVE

TEST 205
AUGUST: It has 31 days; all the other months have 30 days.

TEST 206
BOOK

TEST 207
6. The sum of the numbers in each column decreases by one from left to right (24, 23, 22, 21, 20).

TEST 208
CALIPER (LIP)

TEST 209
D. At each stage an additional line is added, and the figure is reflected.

TEST 210
TELESCOPIC

TEST 211
Zero. There are three white socks and one black sock in the drawer. The chances are as follows:
White pair   =   0.5
Mixed pair   =   0.5
Black pair   =   0

TEST 212
D. RUTCK = TRUCK. The boats are CARAVEL, CANOE, LAUNCH, and CRUISER.

TEST 213
APPEASE

TEST 214
MEAD

TEST 215
KINGFISHER

TEST 216
HAND

TEST 217
NIPPON

TEST 218
PALPATES, EXAMINES

TEST 219
MEAT

TEST 220
E

TEST 221
B doesn't fit.

TEST 222
FELLOWSHIP

TEST 223
B. 71364259. The numbers move from the position ABCDEFGH to the position EGBDAHFC.

TEST 224
ARTISAN = SINATRA. The instruments are
CORNET, BASSOON, PICCOLO, and ACCORDION.

TEST 225
PLETHORA, DEARTH

TEST 226
E. It contains a shaded part common to two figures.
In all the others, the shaded area is common to
only one figure.

TEST 227
3. Starting at 0 and moving two segments clockwise
yields the series 0, 1, ?, 6, 10, 15, 21. The difference
between terms in the series is 1, 2, 3, 4, 5, 6.

TEST 228
OUST

TEST 229
DON'T TAKE CHANCES

TEST 230
MODULATE, REGULATE

TEST 231
726. Each number is produced by adding the
previous number to its reverse. For example, 33 =
12 + 21. 726 = 363 + 363.

TEST 232
Innocent (in O cent)

TEST 233
GIBUS (hat). All the others have to do with horse
legs.

TEST 234
PILLAGE

TEST 235
SILK

TEST 236
WIND

TEST 237
E. RUGAS = SUGAR. The forms of transportation
are TRAIN, OMNIBUS, CYCLE, and TRAM.

TEST 238
TRICKERY

TEST 239
TICK

TEST 240
E

TEST 241
RUMINATE, CONSIDER

TEST 242
ON THE LOOSE

TEST 243
A. The second and third numbers are formed
by adding the number in the middle of the
previous number to the previous number.
For example, 46 + 3469 = 3515, and
51 + 3515 = 3566.

TEST 244
PROFICIENT

TEST 245
SLIP

TEST 246
D. It is the only one that doesn't have an identical
match.

TEST 247
LACE

TEST 248
VEILED

TEST 249
NEOPHYTE (novice). All the others have to do with
the sky, space, and gas.

TEST 250
The smallest number has digits multiplying to 1
and summing to 2, namely 11. The next smallest
has digits multiplying to 2 and summing to 4,
namely 112. So the house number is 11 and there
are at most 111 houses.

TEST 251
B. Each pentagon is made by superimposing the
two pentagons below it and removing overlapping
parts.

TEST 252
8. Each square block of four numbers
totals 20.

TEST 253
HORSE

TEST 254
CRISTATE, TUFTED

TEST 255
SELL, CELL

TEST 256
A. WALLSOW = SWALLOW. The fish are TURBOT,
FLOUNDER, PLAICE, and HADDOCK.

TEST 257
HEART-SHAPED

TEST 258
SLUDGE

TEST 259
MAN

TEST 260
A. Each arm rotates a fixed amount at
each stage.

TEST 261
A. The dot in the top left square moves one corner
counterclockwise at each stage. The dot in the top
right square moves one corner counterclockwise at
each stage. The dot in the bottom left square moves
one corner clockwise at each stage. The dot in the
bottom right square moves one corner clockwise at
each stage.

TEST 262
OTTAWA, PARIS, ATHENS

TEST 263
24. Reverse the previous number and drop the highest digit each time.

TEST 264
PATHETIC

TEST 265
PROFANITY, ABUSE

TEST 266
2. The center number equals the upper left number divided by the upper right number times the lower right number divided by the lower left number. $2 = 6 \div 6 \times 12 \div 6$.

TEST 267
EXTEMPORIZE (improvise). All the others have to do with expanding.

TEST 268
D. In each row and column, the third square is the first and second square superimposed, with overlapping parts removed.

TEST 269
$\frac{3}{13}$

TEST 270
CLASSIFIED

TEST 271
67. Each number is obtained by adding together the digits of the previous number to the previous number. $67 = 56 + 5 + 6$.

TEST 272
KING SALMON

TEST 273
CON

TEST 274
FLORET (small flower). All the others have to do with windows.

TEST 275
NOXIOUS, PERNICIOUS

TEST 276
PERVERSE, PETULANT

TEST 277
A. RANBYD = BRANDY. The animals are TIGER, LEOPARD, BUFFALO, and DONKEY.

TEST 278
INTIMATE

TEST 279
EXAGGERATION

TEST 280
B. It is the only one that doesn't have an identical match.

TEST 281
FREQUENT, SPORADIC

TEST 282
DIABOLICAL

TEST 283
4. The lower right number is the sum of the other two divided by eight. $4 = (18 + 14) \div 8$

TEST 284
CONDUIT, CONDUCT

TEST 285
HYPOTENUSE: This line is connected with triangles; the rest are lines of circles.

TEST 286
E. Each row and column contains one white, one black, and one gray background, and three rings, with one center ring black, one middle ring black, and one outer ring black.

TEST 287

Never. An eternal loop is completed at the fifth stage.

TEST 288
AEGIS, PATRONAGE

TEST 289
My house number is 91, and I am 82 years old. $(91 \times 91 = 8281)$

TEST 290
RECONSTITUTE

TEST 291
SATURATE, PERMEATE

TEST 292
MON

TEST 293
PRIMER

TEST 294
5. The middle number is the product of the top and lower left number divided by the lower right number. $5 = 11 \times 10 \div 22$.

TEST 295
FISH

TEST 296
C. BEZAR = ZEBRA. The birds are FINCH, SPARROW, HAWK, and THRUSH.

TEST 297
BEDBUG

TEST 298
SPRUCE

TEST 299
36. The difference between terms in the series is a series of squares, 4, 9, 16, 25, 36 (2^2, 3^2, 4^2, 5^2, 6^2).

TEST 300
D. In each row and column, the third circle is the first and second circle superimposed, with overlapping parts removed.

STUMPER 1
INCOMPREHENSIBLE

STUMPER 2
30. $7 \times 4 + 2 = 30$

STUMPER 3
PUITN = INPUT

STUMPER 4
D. The figure on the left arm goes inside the figure on the right arm. The remainder of the original goes inside the central figure.

STUMPER 5
WIT, WITLESS, WITNESS

STUMPER 6
All the figures are in anagram pairs except 294, which is therefore the odd one out: 563–635, 916–196, 298–829, 594–945, 752–572, 671–176, 832–283.

STUMPER 7
Laughing all the way to the bank.

STUMPER 8
ALLOT

STUMPER 9
LAUNCH SITE

STUMPER 10
592. The numbers 48375926 are being repeated in the same order.

STUMPER 11
C. Each connected line of four circles contains one each of the four different symbols.

STUMPER 12
Take the bull by the horns.

STUMPER 13
35. The numbers represent the position of each letter T in the sentence.

STUMPER 14
3. The numbers indicated by the hands increase by 7 each time—i.e., 12, 19, 26, 33.

STUMPER 15
NOTABLE, NOT ABLE, NO TABLE

STUMPER 16
D. WET. Each letter moves forward four places in the alphabet.

S	TUV	W
A	BCD	E
P	QRS	T

STUMPER 17
Tower of strength

STUMPER 18
6. Each line of the four circles totals 17.

STUMPER 19
D. A facial feature appears in the center when it appears three times in the surrounding circles.

STUMPER 20
SAPPHIRE. These are all "blue" words.

STUMPER 21
D

STUMPER 22
C. DESPAIR

STUMPER 23
C

STUMPER 24
TUTORIAL

STUMPER 25
MACKEREL

STUMPER 26
$5/11 \div 25/22 = 5/11 \times 22/25 = 2/5$.

STUMPER 27
OVERSHADOW

STUMPER 28
$29/40$. Divide the top and bottom by 25.

STUMPER 29
B. MUSOPHOBIA

STUMPER 30
C. DINNER

STUMPER 31
PITCH

STUMPER 32
36. We use a mathematical base of 10. If we use 8, we get $64 - 8 - 1$. $2 - 0$ (4×4 mod $10 = 16$), but 4×4 mod $8 = 20$. Therefore, $3 - 6$ (5×6 mod $10 = 30$), but 5×6 mod $8 = 36$.

STUMPER 33
C.
A = crypts,
B = lyrics,
D = script.

STUMPER 34
6. In each vertical column the three smaller numbers equal the larger number.

STUMPER 35
D. EXPERT

STUMPER 36
$$44. (8 \times 7) = 56$$
$$- (2 \times 6) = \underline{12}$$
$$= 44$$

STUMPER 37
B. TIERCEL (bird)

STUMPER 38
GUPPY, POPPY

STUMPER 39
C.

STUMPER 40
LOCKJAW

STUMPER 41
SEPTEMBER
ANTISEPTIC
CENTIPEDE
MULTIPLE
JULY

STUMPER 42
22. Each number is derived by adding the two numbers at either side of it.

STUMPER 43
DEFT THEFT

STUMPER 44
MEAT, STEW, TART, SAGO, BEAN, FLAN, RICE.

STUMPER 45
WEDNESDAY

STUMPER 46
3. All the other figures have an arrow pointing to their shortest side.

STUMPER 47

Seven pieces

STUMPER 48
"Many hands make light work."

STUMPER 49
12

STUMPER 50

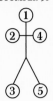

27. Add digits of Circle 2 to obtain Circle 1.
Add digits of Circle 1 to obtain Circle 4.
Multiply digits of Circle 2 to obtain Circle 3.
Multiply digits of Circle 3 to obtain Circle 5.

STUMPER 51
1. All widgets have a hole in the middle.

STUMPER 52
12. $9 \times 8 = 72 \div 6 = 12$.
Therefore, $9 \times 4 = 36 \div 3 = 12$.

STUMPER 53
All are buildings: LODGE (OGLED), TOWER (WROTE), CASTLE (CLEATS), TEMPLE (PELMET).

STUMPER 54
D. In all the others, the rectangle and black dot are at either side of the arrow. In D, it is the white dot and rectangle.

STUMPER 55
$6\frac{1}{4}$. $(5 \times \frac{1}{2}) \times (10 \times \frac{1}{4})$

STUMPER 56
COMANCHERO

STUMPER 57
C. Throbbing

STUMPER 58
MA IS AS SELFLESS AS I AM.

STUMPER 59
C. RISK

STUMPER 60
315. Multiply by 0.75, 0.5, 0.25, and repeat.

STUMPER 61
2. The numbers represent the number of rectangles in which they are inside.

STUMPER 62
GERMANE, COGNATE

STUMPER 63
LYCHEE

STUMPER 64
A. Now each line points to a different side
or corner.

STUMPER 65
JACK

STUMPER 66
$33. Vowels = $4; consonants = $5.

STUMPER 67
8. The corresponding segments of each circle add
up to 19. Example: 6 + 11 + 2 = 19
         7 + 5 + 7 = 19

STUMPER 68
REFEREES. The missing letters are R and F.

STUMPER 69
C. 19.635 sq. in.

STUMPER 70
E. TENDON

STUMPER 71
63. (9 × 9) − (6 × 3)

STUMPER 72
$\frac{1}{12}$;

$$\frac{16 \times 9 \times 7 \times 2}{8 \times 18 \times 14 \times 12} = \frac{2,016}{24,192} = \frac{1}{12}$$

STUMPER 73
It is a wise father that knows his own child.

STUMPER 74
CORSAIR, FELDSPAR

STUMPER 75
C

STUMPER 76
D. The X is midway between a black and white
ball.

STUMPER 77
N and M to spell Enumerate

STUMPER 78
ALLEYWAY

STUMPER 79
ANCESTRY

STUMPER 80
V and F to spell OVERFLOWS

STUMPER 81
THANKSGIVING

STUMPER 82
They all contain the letters ONE in a certain
position:

_ ON _ E _	_ _ ON _ E	_ O _ NE _
LONGER	BLONDE	CORNER
MONKEY	BRONZE	LOANED
WONDER	SPONGE	HORNET

STUMPER 83
Four ways.

STUMPER 84
B. This completes every possible arrangement of
four blocks, not counting rotations and reflections.

STUMPER 85
C. Soft

STUMPER 86
2.

In each pentagon, A + D = E + B + C

STUMPER 87
JOE

STUMPER 88
SACRAMENTO (ESCORT A MAN)

STUMPER 89
OCCUPANT, RESIDENT

STUMPER 90

STUMPER 91
4,146. In all the others, A × C = B and B + C = D.
For example: 3628 = ABCD. 3 × 2 = 6 and
6 + 2 = 8.

STUMPER 92

STUMPER 93
B. The figure is flipped over vertically.

STUMPER 94
ABALONE, ABANDON, ABDICATE, ABDOMEN, ABOUND, ABROGATES, ABSCOND

STUMPER 95
RUSH

STUMPER 96
AC(CORD)IAN

STUMPER 97
ENERGETIC, LETHARGIC

STUMPER 98
12. Add up the three numbers and reverse—i.e., $7 + 8 + 6 = 21$.

STUMPER 99
SLACK, TIGHT

STUMPER 100
D. The final figure at the end of each row and column is determined by the contents of the previous two squares. When a symbol appears in the same place in both squares it is carried forward but changes from cross to dot, and vice versa.

STUMPER 101
FIFE, TUBA, LUTE, OBOE. ODD PAIR: HA

STUMPER 102
32. Simplify: $5 + (8 \div 4) + (9 \times 2) + 7 = 5 + 2 + 18 + 7 = 32$ Order of operations: $\times \div + -$

STUMPER 103
PINION

STUMPER 104
JERKIN

STUMPER 105
JOSH, TEASE

STUMPER 106
C. This contains the only ice-cream-cone-shaped figure that has two black circles in it.

STUMPER 107
A

STUMPER 108
BERBERIS, CAPSICUM, FOXGLOVE

STUMPER 109
CONE (NICK) KRIS
1 2   2413 3 4
LISP (SOLE) ETON
1 2   2413 3 4

STUMPER 110
C. 400 ft. ($5^2 \times 16 = 400$)

STUMPER 111
44. Start at 24, then add 6, then deduct 4, spiralling in towards the center.

STUMPER 112
B. 720.
Take pi as $^{22}/_7$; then, $^{22}/_7 \times 28 = 88$ inches = $\dfrac{1760 \times 3 \times 12}{88} = 720$

STUMPER 113
⊢ They are numbers 1 to 8 with the top and bottom horizontal lines missing.

STUMPER 114
B. ∞

STUMPER 115
CHRISTMAS, MAURITIUS, FALKLAND

STUMPER 116
TEN

STUMPER 117
C

STUMPER 118
CABBAGE

STUMPER 119
DECK. QUARTERDECK, DECKHAND

STUMPER 120
D

STUMPER 121
F. All those with one black eye have their curl to the right. All those with a black nose have their curl to the left. All those with neither black eye nor nose have their curl pointing straight up.

STUMPER 122
INTELLIGENTLY

STUMPER 123
AGE-GROUP, STOCK-STILL, BLOOD-TYPING, TWIN-SIZE

STUMPER 124
Minus $100

STUMPER 125
LEAST

STUMPER 126
1. The top line plus the bottom line equal the middle line, i.e., $5384968 + 3276873 = 8661841$.

STUMPER 127

B. AGATHA, to complete the sequence:

_ A _ _ B _
_ C _ _ D _
_ E _ _ F _
_ G _ _ H _

STUMPER 128

LET THE CAT OUT OF THE BAG

STUMPER 129

C

STUMPER 130

10 provinces in Canada

STUMPER 131

ARMADA
WARMTH
CHARMS
DISARM

XYZ = ARM

STUMPER 132

8. The sum of each column of numbers increases by 1 each time.

STUMPER 133

STUMPER 134

G and T to spell ORIGINATOR

STUMPER 135

A. It has only one loose end; the others all have two.

STUMPER 136

1. CAPACITY
2. BRAIN
3. EXPLORING
4. LEARNED

STUMPER 137

PENELOPE

STUMPER 138

812. 6 + 2 = 8; 9 + 3 = 12

STUMPER 139

RETORTS (ORBIT) LIBERTY
2 5 1   12345 43

STUMPER 140

A bolt from the blue

STUMPER 141

20. 6, 5, 2, 3, 4. Opposite sides always add up to 7.

STUMPER 142

E. A is the same as C; B is the same as D.

STUMPER 143

B. SAMOYED (dog). The others are: A. QUETZALE, C. CRUSADO, D. BOLIVAR, E. TESTER, F. SESTERCE.

STUMPER 144

COASTER

STUMPER 145

HERMIT, NAUSEA

STUMPER 146

JITTERBUG, QUADRILLE, POLONAISE

STUMPER 147

LADYLIKE, HOYDENISH

STUMPER 148

SLUGGISH, INACTIVE. The missing letters are: s, g, c, and v.

STUMPER 149

E. BOAT

STUMPER 150

x. Add 2 + 4 + 4 = 10 = X

STUMPER 151

11½. There are two series

(+1½)
7
8 ½
10
11½

(−2 ¾)
17
14 ¼
11½

STUMPER 152

E. SCARF

STUMPER 153

A. ICOSAHEDRON

STUMPER 154

D. 120°.

$$\frac{360°}{6} = 60° = \text{Central Angle.} \quad 180° − 60° = 120°.$$

STUMPER 155

$$-2. \frac{(4 \times 2) - 6}{7 - (4 \times 2)} = \frac{2}{-1} = -2$$

STUMPER 156
E. CATS

STUMPER 157
RED

STUMPER 158
SOUBRETTE

STUMPER 159
C. A = PRIZES; B = Crepes or creeps;
D = Precis or prices

STUMPER 160
E. Food

STUMPER 161
MAT

✳ between words means anagram

➤ between words means add a letter

★ between words means change first letter

STUMPER 162
They all contain names of animals: A(MULE)T,
D(EMU)RE, MO(RAT)ORIUM, MUL(TIGER)M

STUMPER 163
A. This completes every possible permutation of
the original square where none of the four symbols
occupy the position they held in the original square.

STUMPER 164
B. ESCAPADE

STUMPER 165
ICEBREAKER

STUMPER 166
He loved Vienna. He hated places whose names are
made up of two three-letter words: MAD-RID,
WAR-SAW, ANT-RIM.

STUMPER 167
21. All the others are in 1:3 ratio pairs:15–45, 9–27,
18–54, 8–24.

STUMPER 168

8	6	2
4	T	7
5	1	3

STUMPER 169
VICUNA. All the others are man-made.

STUMPER 170
SLIDE RULE/SLY DROOL

STUMPER 171
RECLAIM, MIRACLE

STUMPER 172
7.

14		11
2	6	
⑦	4	10

STUMPER 173
B. The medium-size rectangle is moving from
left to right at each stage.

STUMPER 174
WATER, MOVEMENT

STUMPER 175
G. Start at the left-side letter R and jump clockwise
to alternate segments to spell out the word
"regular."

STUMPER 176
C. It is a mirror image of the opposite square.

STUMPER 177
Nine. Thirty-one people pay $2.27 each. 9 × 31 =
$70.37.

STUMPER 178
PEACE

STUMPER 179
3,205

STUMPER 180

E D O	F P B	S I O N
H E B M	M Y I	A M O A
S E A T	O T M A	S R O T

Start at the letter indicated and spiral clockwise
around the perimeter to spell out "mashed potato."

STUMPER 181
A

STUMPER 182
KHAKI, IGUANA

STUMPER 183
A. .857. They read as follows: $\frac{1}{2}$, $\frac{2}{3}$, $\frac{3}{4}$, $\frac{4}{5}$, $\frac{5}{6}$, $\frac{6}{7}$.

STUMPER 184
E. BALE

STUMPER 185
DUNLIN

STUMPER 186
$\frac{6}{7}$. $\frac{1}{3} \div \frac{7}{18} = \frac{1}{3} \times \frac{18}{7} = \frac{6}{7}$.

STUMPER 187
C. The other examples comprise pairs of numbers and one of their factors.
A. $13 \times 4 = 52$
$37 \times 10 = 370$
$23 \times 5 = 115$
B. $22 \times 4 = 88$
$16 \times 7 = 112$
$17 \times 8 = 136$
C. $15 \times 6 = 90$
$24 \times 6 = 144$
$19 \times 10 = 190$, not 290

STUMPER 188
1. S; it is the only letter not made of straight lines.
2. N; it is the only letter made up of straight lines.
3. D; it is the only letter not made of straight lines.

STUMPER 189
C. CALABASH (fruit)

STUMPER 190
MISSEL THRUSH

STUMPER 191

The circles are in sets of three in different orders:

STUMPER 192
SLOWWORM

STUMPER 193
A. HODOPHOBIA

STUMPER 194
CUR, RAT, APE

STUMPER 195
C. 108°. $\frac{360°}{5} = 72° =$ Central Angle.

$180° - 72° = 108°$.

STUMPER 196
$3\frac{1}{2}$. $(5 \times \frac{1}{10}) + (12 \times \frac{1}{4})$

STUMPER 197
INGRAINED

STUMPER 198
$1365 = \dfrac{15 \times 14 \times 13 \times 12 \times 11 \times 10 \times 9 \times 8 \times 7 \times 6 \times 5}{1 \times 2 \times 3 \times 4 \times 5 \times 6 \times 7 \times 8 \times 9 \times 10 \times 11}$

STUMPER 199
L is the same number of letters away from E & S; B & V; G & Q

STUMPER 200
0.375

STUMPER 201

C	M	A	G	I
A	G	I	C	M
I	C	M	A	G
M	A	G	I	C
G	I	C	M	A

STUMPER 202
Hit the nail on the head.

STUMPER 203
30 mph.
210 miles $\div$ 30 = 7 hours
210 miles $\div$ 35 = 6 hours

STUMPER 204
D. The rest are all the same figure rotated.

STUMPER 205
8. Looking along each row and down each column the sums of alternate numbers are the same. For example: $9 + 6 = 4 + 11$; $9 + 5 = 3 + 11$.

STUMPER 206
STUDY

STUMPER 207
GAUNT

STUMPER 208
IDENTICALLY ELECTING POET

STUMPER 209
SEPTEMBER. Start at JANUARY and jump one month, then two months, then three months, etc.

STUMPER 210
R. Take the left-hand letter from the top row and the right-hand letter from the bottom row added to ATE to spell EATEN. Then work left to right on the top and right to left on the bottom to spell out the words: EATEN, WATER, LATEX, HATED, DATED, GATES, and CATER.

STUMPER 211

D. Working counterclockwise around the larger circles, the shaded quadrant moves one place clockwise. Working clockwise round the smaller circles, the shaded quadrant moves one place counterclockwise.

STUMPER 212

150.
$38 \times 2 \ (+2) = 78$
$39 \times 2 \ (+2) = 80$
$58 \times 2 \ (+2) = 118$
$74 \times 2 \ (+2) = 150$

STUMPER 213

FACULTY

STUMPER 214

24. The numbers, spelled out, follow the numerical sequence: 3-4-5-6-7-8-9-10. One, four, seven, eleven, fifteen, thirteen, seventeen. So the answer is 24—i.e., twenty-four = 10 letters.

STUMPER 215

GEORGINA. REIN AGOG is an anagram of Georgina; REAR LION is an anagram of Lorraine.

STUMPER 216

B. In all the others the outer figure is the same as the inner figure.

STUMPER 217

A. The red ball

STUMPER 218

ODD ONE OUT

STUMPER 219

STRATAGEM

STUMPER 220

MENDELSSOHN

STUMPER 221

77. After the third number, each number is the total of the three preceding numbers.

STUMPER 222

5. $6 \times 9 = 54$
$54 - 5 = 49$
Similarly, $(7 \times 4) - 4 = 24$
$(3 \times 9) - 8 = 19$

STUMPER 223

APSE.

ROPE	(PART)	ANTE
3 1	1234	2 4
SHAM	(APSE)	PIER
3 1	1234	2 4

STUMPER 224

15. We use a mathematical base of 10. If we use 7, we get $49 - 7 - 1$. Therefore, $2 - 4 \ (3 \times 6$ mod $10 = 18$), but 3×6 mod $7 = 24$. $1 - 5 \ (4 \times 3$ mod $10 = 12$), but 4×3 mod $7 = 15$.

STUMPER 225

5.

$$\frac{24}{1 + 4 + 3} = 3$$

$$\frac{18}{1 + 4 + 1} = 3$$

$$\frac{30}{1 + 4 + 5} = 3$$

STUMPER 226

HILDEGARDE

STUMPER 227

POACH

STUMPER 228

C. 10

STUMPER 229

MONEYMAKER

STUMPER 230

ODIOUS, MURDER

STUMPER 231

D.

STUMPER 232

$7^1/_2$. There are two series:
$(+ 2^1/_4) \quad 1 \ 3^1/_4 \ 5^1/_2 \ 7^3/_4$
$(-1^1/_2) \quad 12 \ 10^1/_2 \ 9 \ 7^1/_2$

STUMPER 233

ROUGHCAST

STUMPER 234

$^{27}/_{40}$. Divide the top and bottom by 25.

STUMPER 235

ADELE, ANNIE, ELIZA, ERICA

STUMPER 236

FUZZY-WUZZY

STUMPER 237

SIGNALMAN, GONDOLIER, MANNEQUIN

STUMPER 238

The numbers increase by 1, 2, 3, etc. The difference between the letters is 2, 3, 5 and 8, respectively, according to the number in the preceding diamond.

STUMPER 239

PIN

STUMPER 240

B. 15

STUMPER 241

STUMPER 242

RECONDITE, DARK

STUMPER 243

SUPPORTER, ADVERSARY

STUMPER 244

B.

A = DOE (EVIL-DOERS)
C = BEAR (BE ARMED)
D = EWE (BEJEWELLED)
E = APE (TRAP EASILY)

STUMPER 245

310. Looking around the circles: $\dot{2}\dot{5}$ and $\dot{3}\dot{2}$ = 84
by adding 5 + 3 = 8
        2 + 2 = 4
$\dot{3}\dot{2}$ and $\dot{7}\dot{3}$ = 96
by adding 2 + 7 = 9
        3 + 3 = 6
$\dot{7}\dot{3}$ and $\dot{5}\dot{1}$ = 88
by adding 3 + 5 = 8
        7 + 1 = 8
Therefore: $\dot{5}\dot{1}$ + $\dot{2}\dot{5}$ = 310
by adding 1 + 2 = 3
        5 + 5 = 10

STUMPER 246

B.

STUMPER 247

CLEAVER. It is a cutting tool whereas the rest are drilling tools.

STUMPER 248

C.

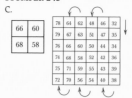

Move from 32 to 78 by the route shown in the sequence: + 3, − 1, + 2.

STUMPER 249

MUESLI

STUMPER 250

All have two meanings when spelled the same but pronounced differently: APPROPRIATE (take possession of, suitable) BOW (and arrow, to the King) DESERT (leave alone, Sahara) DOVE (dived, bird) ENTRANCE (door, delight) GILL (unit of volume, organ of fish) LEAD (pipe, astray) SLAVER (slave trader, drool)

STUMPER 251

9.

5 × 3 = 15   3 × 9 = 27
6 × 2 = 12
        ———
        27

STUMPER 252

B. The top half is folded over onto the bottom half.

STUMPER 253

C. The shaded figures represent 0.75 and 0.5.
72 × 0.5 = 36
68 × 0.75 = 51

STUMPER 254

HERE, THERE

STUMPER 255

TOR. OPERATOR, TORUS.

STUMPER 256

CROSS-EXAMINATION

STUMPER 257

CHARLESTON

STUMPER 258
37.5 minutes.

$$\frac{50 \times 6}{8} = \frac{300}{8} = 37.5$$

STUMPER 259
D. The third counter from the top disappears at each stage.

STUMPER 260
OFFICIOUS

STUMPER 261
B. SILK FABRIC

STUMPER 262
ALUMINUM, MAGNESIUM , MANGANESE

STUMPER 263
DEPRESSED

STUMPER 264
A. REEL, so that it spells: 1-2-3. S<u>ON</u>, <u>EA</u>T, <u>WORTH</u>, <u>R</u>EEL.

STUMPER 265
C

STUMPER 266
D and E. They cannot be folded into a cube.

STUMPER 267
(C) ZINC

STUMPER 268
VOLATILE

STUMPER 269
OBSTETRICS

STUMPER 270
HOTELIER. The missing letters are H and L.

STUMPER 271
142. The differences are:

1×19	2×19	3×19
19	38	57
4×19	5×19	6×19
76	95	114

STUMPER 272
Here today, gone tomorrow.

STUMPER 273
4. Subtract the sum of the outside numbers from the sum of the inside ones.
$(6 + 7 + 7 + 4) - (2 + 1 + 9 + 8)$

STUMPER 274
RED

STUMPER 275
PADDLING

STUMPER 276
(D) IRREVERENCE

STUMPER 277
WINTER CHERRY

STUMPER 278
JALOPY

STUMPER 279
The family that prays together stays together.

STUMPER 280
9.
$$\frac{3 \times 7 \times 3}{7}$$

STUMPER 281
A. The dot moves down at each stage, first jumping one square, then two, then three. A square turns black once it has been visited by the dot.

STUMPER 282
11. The right-hand circle contains the sum of pairs of digits from the three- figure number in the left-hand circle and vice versa—
i.e., 378. $3 + 7 = 10$; $3 + 8 = 11$; $7 + 8 = 15$.

STUMPER 283
SPEND, HOARD

STUMPER 284
GRIDIRON, WORKLOAD, FIREWOOD, MAINLAND

STUMPER 285
468137. The even numbers and then odd numbers from the first number are placed in ascending order to form the second number.

STUMPER 286
They all contain the names of countries:
L<u>IBERA</u>TION: IRAN; <u>INITIALL</u>Y: ITALY;
F<u>RAGRANCE</u>: FRANCE; <u>CHINCHILLA</u>: CHINA;
<u>SPEARMINT</u>: SPAIN; <u>PERFUME</u>: PERU;
CLAUS<u>TROPHOBIA</u>: AUSTRIA

STUMPER 287
W. It has twenty-two letters in the alphabet before it, and three letters after it.

STUMPER 288
GATEMAN'S NAME TAG

STUMPER 289
SPRING

STUMPER 290
Bend over backwards

STUMPER 291
2. Looking both across and down, the sum of each pair of numbers is one more than that of the previous pair of numbers.

STUMPER 292
XYZ = RAP. RAPIDS, DRAPES, SCRAPE, ENTRAP

STUMPER 293
LONE, LOAN

STUMPER 294
F, J, J, N. They are the initial letters of the months of the year.

STUMPER 295
MINUET. All the words are dances.

STUMPER 296
D. All the others are made up of three identical figures; D is made up of four

STUMPER 297
VANISH

STUMPER 298
GENEROUS, CHARITABLE, BENEVOLENT, KIND

STUMPER 299
IMPRISONMENT. The missing letters are P, N, and T.

STUMPER 300
LLAMA, SKATE

STUMPER 301
MINE: MINERAL, EMINENT

STUMPER 302
SPITEFUL

STUMPER 303
B. EXCITING. Each word commences with the last letter of the previous word.

STUMPER 304
PAJAMA

STUMPER 305
0.875

STUMPER 306
D. ULNA

STUMPER 307
HOSPITABLE

STUMPER 308
(C) ENTRAILS

STUMPER 309
AGE

STUMPER 310
C. Cr

STUMPER 311
CLUTTER

STUMPER 312
HAMBURGER, MINCEMEAT, SPAGHETTI

STUMPER 313
(E) DISAPPROVAL

STUMPER 314
TOKEN.

BATH	SALTS
GREEN	PEPPERS
ICE	FLOE
MAGIC	SQUARE

STUMPER 315
E. DUMPLINGS

STUMPER 316
D. DEACON

STUMPER 317
B. PICTURE POSTCARDS

STUMPER 318
2 hours. $6 \text{ hrs} = \dfrac{1}{6} = .167$

$3 \text{ hrs} = \dfrac{1}{3} = .333$

$.167 + .333 = 0.5$

$\dfrac{1}{0.5} = 2$

STUMPER 319
C. CLUB SHAPED

STUMPER 320
52. $(12 \times 5) = 60 - (4 \times 2) = 52$